BOBBY MOORE

BOBBY MOORE

THE ILLUSTRATED BIOGRAPHY OF A FOOTBALLING LEGEND

EDITED BY DAVID EMERY
Daily Express SPORTS EDITOR

HEADLINE

First published in 1993
by HEADLINE BOOK PUBLISHING PLC

10 9 8 7 6 5 4 3 2 1

ISBN 0 7472 7867 9

Book Interior by Design/Section

Illustration reproduction by Koford, Singapore

Printed and bound in Great Britain
by BPCC Hazells Ltd, Member of BPCC Ltd

HEADLINE BOOK PUBLISHING PLC
Headline House
79 Great Titchfield Street
London W1P 7FN

CONTENTS

ACKNOWLEDGEMENTS

The authors would like to thank other members of the *Daily Express* Sports Department who helped make the book possible: Peter Tozer, Ian Cole, Kevin Moseley and Mike Allen. Also editorial and production personnel at Headline Book Publishing for their hard work.
The authors would like to thank Ron Greenwood, too, for providing the foreword. Mr Greenwood has asked for his fee to be paid to the Imperial Cancer Research Fund.

FOREWORD

BY RON GREENWOOD
FORMER ENGLAND AND WEST HAM MANAGER

Bobby Moore was skill personified and a model captain. From a manager's point of view, he was an ideal player and, during his time, he vied with Franz Beckenbauer for the title of the world's greatest defender.

He set out to become a perfectionist and this he achieved. He was not a naturally gifted player. He had to work at it. And work he did.

The man had such stature in the game: a marvellous ambassador for English football, a leader but not a bossy one. He did not rant or rave. He rarely raised his voice. But he had a wonderful way with players.

I first saw him play for London Schoolboys against Glasgow Schoolboys in an Under-15 match at Stamford Bridge. He stood out even then. He had a cultured look. I made a mental note of him as you do when you are impressed with a youngster.

I was manager of Eastbourne United before becoming manager of England Youth, the beginnings of our relationship. He skippered that side and later England Under-21s, when I was also in charge.

It is not generally known that he postponed becoming a full professional at West Ham so he could captain the England Youth side in the European Championships. This was typical of his attitude and the pride he felt about playing for his country, qualities that never left him. They were never more evident than when he lifted the World Cup.

I became assistant manager at Arsenal before taking charge at West Ham, where he had just broken into the first team. He was a pleasure to work with and had such a thirst for knowledge. He represented everything we believed in: how the game should be played; how players should conduct themselves.

Perhaps his outstanding moment for the club was when he won the European Cup-Winners' Cup, beating Munich 1860 at Wembley in 1965. West Ham showed England could compete with, and beat, the best in Europe. The next year, of course, we showed we could do the same on a world stage. And he reflected the glory in that achievement.

When he was taken from us it was almost as if a certain set of standards had passed away, too, such was his influence and impression on us all. He holds so many fond memories.

PART ONE

BOBBY MOORE

THE EARLY YEARS

BY CHRISTOPHER HILTON

CHAPTER ONE

THE SCHOOLBOY WITH A DREAM

Acold but gentle breeze plucked at the scarves draped with such care and in such profusion over the gate. A middle-aged woman stooped to set down a bunch of flowers among the many which spread from the foot of the gate. She turned, tears welling in her eyes and moved quickly away. Perhaps 50 or 60 people milled awkwardly, gazing at the scarves and the flowers and the touching, hand-written messages on home-made boards hung here and there. Each represented a cry from the heart. The few people who spoke did so in hushed whispers, as if in the presence of something overwhelming.

This was the scene at Upton Park, on Saturday morning, 27 February 1993, just a few days after the death of Bobby Moore.

Those who milled around each nursed their own particular memories; some remembered the tubby 16-year-old who came to West Ham as a kid among kids and within a year captained the England Youth side; others looked back to the great years, the Cup final of 1964 and the European Cup-Winners' Cup final in 1965. There were memories of his 108 international caps and of that July afternoon at Wembley in 1966 which everybody remembers, and the extra-time pass which dropped so exquisitely for Geoff Hurst to score the fourth goal against West Germany. It was the moment that BBC commentator Kenneth Wolstenholme captured in the words everybody remembers: 'There are spectators on the pitch. They think it's all over. It is now …'

To hear these words echo in the memory – as they do – remains poignant, but not so poignant as February 1993 and that gate. It was all over now, a life so enriching which began a comfortable bus ride away and began, literally, with a bang.

Robert Frederick Moore was born in the front bedroom of 43 Waverley Gardens, Barking on 12 April 1941, the only child of Robert Edward and Doris. All locals of a certain age remember the date. That night, German bombs hammered down the largest shop in Barking, known as Blake's Corner and a famous landmark.

Moore Senior worked as an electrician at the local power station and hastened home to see his son. Quickly, he made a decision: paternity leave was completely unknown, particularly in wartime, but he couldn't very well leave his wife and new-born baby alone in the house while he went back to work, especially as the Luftwaffe were coming over in waves. He found transport from somewhere and took them to her mother's house a mile away.

Mrs Doris Frome lived opposite. 'Don't forget in those times we were all living in bomb shelters in the back gardens. I got up about six in the morning and said, "I'm going across to see how Mrs Moore is with her new baby." I knocked and couldn't get any answer. Along came the midwife to take care of them and asked if I had been able to get an answer. I hadn't, but just then his dad returned from the night shift. "It's all right, Mrs Frome," he said. "I've taken them out to her mother's." He had to. We were getting daylight raids all the time, too.'

The midwife, Josephine Lawson, a 22-year-old, was born in Cumbria and was training to be both midwife and general district nurse. She recalls that she went down to Plaistow Maternity Hospital, which was later evacuated and subsequently bombed out. 'I did a case book on births, all the information you needed, mother's age, whether it's the first baby or second, and so on. I nursed mothers for 14 days after the birth, until they were back on their feet. I don't think I was actually there at Bobby's birth. Of course it was such a long time ago and just one of hundreds that I dealt with, but seeing it in all the newspapers and on the television when he died must have rung some kind of bell. I got my old case book out to confirm it and there he was …'

The cities in wartime Britain could be sparse, damaged, darkened places – no lights at night which might tell the bombers what lay below them – and those members of each community who hadn't been evacuated drew together and fashioned a mutual warmth, a strong resilience to adversity. Waverley Gardens was one such, a typical and completely unremarkable suburban street of the kind which spread out from London in a vast maze. Built in the 1930s, the terraced houses featured shallow, arched brick entrances masking the front doors, pebble-dashed walls and, as a gesture to style, triangular gables above the front bedroom window. And it was there that Bobby was born.

'He was a dear little soul,' Mrs Frome says. 'I remember him always kicking a ball in the road as a child. It came into my garden often enough and I'd say "Bobby, take that ball somewhere else", but really he was no trouble. A good boy, but most kids were then. With the air raids going on they weren't allowed to stray far and they were kept under control. In fact, his mother was pretty strict with him, although he was the only child. She called him Robert, the only one who did. He was Bobby to everyone else. Dad was a very nice man, an ordinary man, civil, quiet as his mother was. They were simply quiet, ordinary folk. She must have been very proud of him when he got on in his career but she never let it show.'

In the life of every man, some influences run deep. In the paragraph above Mrs Frome used the word 'quiet' twice. The repetition is no accident and this tendency was soon to be reinforced. In time, Moore would go about his business quietly, whether making and keeping friendships, or worrying that after England won the World Cup his hands were dirty and how could he shake the Queen's white gloves with them like that? In the noise of a life lived on the baying, raw, tumultuous stage of football, he kept his silence and simply played. It gave him a stature that touched millions in Britain, even among the most vehement, tribal supporters of opposition teams; it touched many millions more during the World Cup because he stayed true to the honesty of his background and never considered becoming the type of man he was not. He might be in Mexico but he was from Waverley Gardens, Barking.

'He really was the boy next door,' Mrs Frome says. 'If he saw me he'd say "Hello, how are you?" Polite, you see. I remember, too, how he never hurried when he walked down the street but seemed to glide. I suppose naturally athletic people do that.'

He went to a nearby school, Westbury, and began to play for a local Saturday morning side, South Park Boys, in the Ilford League. Dennis Allen, a member and one of the famous footballing family, remembers clearly when Moore and a schoolfriend from Westbury joined. 'I was eleven and Bobby ten. His friend lived in the same road as I did, along with Terry Venables and Ken Brown, who was also at West Ham. We all lived in Bonham Road.' The tight-knit community spirit had continued into peacetime.

'I played midfield and Bobby played centre half in the old-fashioned sense. When he first came, we thought it funny because he was short and a little bit tubby. But he was a good player … well, a brilliant player. He was very quiet, very, very quiet, and kept himself to himself. He was already the person so many people came to know later on. He had the same mannerisms, a certain air about him. He ran with a stiff back and his head up high. He seemed better at everything than everybody else; he was a good cricketer as well …'

They were happy, traditional, innocent days. The 'manager' of South Park, Leonard Lilley, invited the boys round to his house one night a week where they'd play snooker and he'd pick the team for the Saturday. There are no records of how Moore, who attended these informal evenings, played snooker, but we must assume he did it well. From tying a bow tie to passing to Geoff Hurst he did everything well!

'You could see he was going to be great,' Allen says. 'I accept that it's almost unbelievable to say that, but we've been saying it for years. Mind you, at first when he played centre half he'd jump about. No matter where the ball was he'd be jumping around after it; he'd be on his backside getting dirty and not saying a word, just getting on with everything and loving it. He'd dive here and dive there – you'd see him on the ground all the time. He gradually got out of those habits.

'He was a bit like Jimmy Greaves, but in a different way. When Greaves first played he'd never pass to anyone and didn't score many goals. Like Moore, he too had to grow out of these bad early habits. We played against a team called Huntsman's Sports from

The smile is unmistakable, so is the pose. Bobby Moore holds the Barking Primary Schools Championship shield, the first of so many trophies.

Hainault, Essex, in the Ilford League. One day there was a little kid in their side by the name of Greaves and he played against Bobby. I don't know if Jimmy remembers it and I don't know if he realises Bobby was centre half that day. Jimmy played midfield and ran everywhere with the ball. You'd never get it off him, he'd dribble all over the pitch and he'd dribble everything.'

This is a tantalising glimpse of what was to come: Moore, captive of the exuberance of being a ten-year-old; Greaves, captive of the ability to seize a ball and, nimbly, keep it for himself. Only in retrospect does the glimpse assume monumental proportions: Moore eventually grew to the point where he's in everybody's World XI to play Mars, and Greaves, who struck like a viper at goal if he had a yard of space in the penalty area and could make any team in the world look vulnerable. However, the reality in 1951 was that Moore and Greaves were simply a couple of anonymous youngsters among many, many thousands in their area alone. Even today, the broad acres by Hackney marshes, for example, seethe with weekend games as far as the eye can see.

In 1951, with the country only just emerging from post-war rationing and the cities still bearing their bomb sites, choice of entertainment wasn't something kids really had. Rugby represented a middle-class grammar school pastime played somewhere else, not Barking, golf was virtually unknown, athletics was comparatively small-time, and so forth. Life was simple: in winter you, and everybody around you, played soccer in the street and on Saturday for some cosy little team; in summer you played cricket in the street – wickets chalked on walls or, if you had one handy, a lamp-post – and on Saturday for some other cosy little team. If you nursed dreams of making a career of it, the odds against were daunting. No matter. Moore already had a lot going for him.

'Bobby was very, very clever,' Allen says. 'He liked to beat people every time they tried to tackle him – he really was too clever for them. He'd get the ball and pass it. At South Park we had two sides and he played a year above himself, so to speak. I was captain because of being that year older than him. However, he'd drop down to the younger team and captain them if they had an important cup tie, to make sure they got through to the next round. He'd win everything for the younger team – that's how good he was already – then come back and play for us. He left after three years because he started getting known a bit. He played for Leyton Schools and his own school as well – a lot of games. Then Essex began selecting him for Saturday morning games, so he had to leave us.'

On 9 September 1952, Moore went to the Tom Hood Technical High School in Leyton, a typically Victorian two-storey edifice – a third storey was added during his years there. Joan Wright was a teacher who signed Moore's attendance record and she can recall what he was like in those far-off days: 'A bit of a heart-throb, quite frankly, a good-looking lad and sports mad. While at his junior school he'd represented Leyton and Essex. He'd done very well there so he came to us with a little bit of glory attached to him. He was equally good at cricket and played for the local schoolboys team. I am almost sure he played for Essex Schools and everybody at the school wondered which direction he'd choose, soccer or cricket.'

Essex CCC has, understandably, a hazy record of matches so long ago, but people there speak of Moore and another Hammer, Frank Lampard, as players who might well have gone further if they hadn't chosen football instead. It seems certain that Moore played a time or two for the Club and Ground, an invitation team (which no longer exists) composed of schoolboys and those already on the County staff. This was seen as

representing the county and was a considerable honour. There is also a measure of agreement that he represented Essex Boys, too.

Bobby top scores with 64 as West Ham make 196 against Ilford in a charity cricket match. But for once it was a losing captain's performance.

We do know that years later he played for a side organised by Essex coach Frank Rist, who'd also been a footballer. 'We went round playing matches for charity, you'd have the Essex men like Keith Fletcher and Bobby and Geoff Hurst all involved. Bobby batted three or four and, while you can never be sure what might have happened if he'd reached County level, I judged him a top-class club player. He really could bat. He was an excellent fielder anywhere. People say he lacked speed – well, he compensated by anticipation. He even kept wicket from time to time and did that well, too. I formed the impression he could do anything.'

But this all remained in the future. Joan Wright recalls his days at the Tom Hood school: 'Thousands of children have passed through my hands, but I can remember him quite vividly. He became a prefect although never head boy. He didn't see eye-to-eye with the deputy head. She was a spinster. Need I say more? With everyone else he was very popular. Tom Hood was a technical and commercial school where courses would range from book-keeping and typing to woodwork and metalwork rather than Greek and Latin. He did extremely well and, if I remember rightly, passed eight O-levels in one go.

'In later years I used that to some effect. You have pupils who want to become footballers and think they don't have to try much at their academic work. I'd point to the example of Bobby Moore and tell them it is quite possible to do both.'

At Tom Hood he came under the sympathetic gaze of the PE teacher, the late Terry Wilkinson, who also taught geography and was a very keen footballer who'd played for Brentford. (Later, Wilkinson would become a distinguished member of the Sports Council before he died of Parkinson's Disease. A Trust Fund in his memory is currently raising funds to help the disabled take part in sport and recreation; you have the measure of the man in that.)

What precisely Wilkinson, then a slight 22-year-old, saw in Moore we can never know now but all are agreed that he saw something powerful. His widow Maureen says: 'I was a teacher too and it's funny because I also taught someone who achieved fame in later life: the actor Derek Jacobi. Terry and I often talked about it. We decided that you don't spot genius, it comes up and hits you right between the eyes. Bobby, incidentally, was quite fat, puppy fat which he shed.'

Quite how West Ham became actively interested in him is lost now. The manager, Ted Fenton, and the chief scout, Wally St Pier, are both dead but it was a man called Jack Turner – who did some scouting, handled property for the club and advised players financially – who submitted the very first report on Moore. It wasn't particularly favourable. Fenton, who must have heard verbal assessments on the dense East London grapevine, sent Turner back to have another look and reportedly sent others to have a look.

Charles Korr, who has written an extensive history of West Ham, forcibly suggests that the 'final decision' to sign Moore came as a result of the club's failure to sign another promising youngster – he, whoever he was, went to Arsenal. The club could not be seen to be missing out on yet more local talent. For generations, the Cearns family owned West Ham and ran it benevolently, never interfering. But the question across all those years would always be: how ambitious was the club? Was it content to chug along, year after year in great harmony, enjoying the football but going nowhere in particular? Since the war they'd been in the Second Division and, worse, among the players they missed were Venables and Greaves. Inevitably, this must have made them sensitive to missing any more. This was, perhaps, why Fenton took no chances and sent Turner back, covering himself by sending others.

Maureen Wilkinson recaptures the times. 'West Ham scouts were everywhere, watching the schools matches on Saturday mornings and so were Leyton Orient and Arsenal. I don't know if someone rang West Ham and spoke to them about Bobby – if they did they wouldn't say, anyway – or if a West Ham scout just noticed him. When West Ham wanted to sign him his parents came to Terry for advice. He said: " Yes, let him sign, but be careful and read the small print." It was sensible to ask Terry, his schoolteacher, for advice and, of course, Terry had had some experience because he'd played for Brentford.'

Moore left the Tom Hood Technical High School on 19 July 1957. A week later, however, he returned to be presented with an important award, given annually for the pupil who had done most for the school. 'Sometimes it was for academic excellence,' Joan Wright says. 'Sometimes, say, for children who'd done theatre work. Bobby won it for his sporting achievements.' The folklore at the school is quite clear: the day he received it – 24 July 1957 – he was visibly moved. 'He'd been at the school for five years but didn't stay for the sixth. I am sure he was astute enough to have his plans for becoming a professional footballer and in his own way felt he didn't need to go on to higher education. He didn't attempt to take his A-levels.'

CHAPTER TWO

THE GROUNDSTAFF BOY

He went to West Ham as a groundstaff boy and thereby hangs a completely different judgement of his abilities. It comes from a delightful Irishman, Noel Cantwell, who'd joined West Ham in 1952 and would get close to Moore. 'With Bobby living in Barking it would have been quite easy for someone to recommend him but, as you might say, Bobby wasn't an outstanding player as a youngster.'

This means not outstanding to the likes of Cantwell, who naturally surveyed him from a higher level and measured him against higher expectations. It's an old story that the boy who dominates other schoolboys because he's bigger or stronger or better (and often all three) does so because the context is utterly misleading. Because so many people play, there will be many who dominate in their area – that is a statistical certainty. But you only really start to know how good someone is when a club gets its hands on them and pits their dominant players against each other, and even that is no guarantee. As we shall see, a deeply depressing number of the England youth team – itself a high level of promise and what ought, theoretically, to be the highest level of it – vanish without trace.

'Bobby joined us,' Cantwell says. 'He, Geoff Hurst and Martin Peters all came together in a little group when West Ham decided on a youth policy. West Ham challenged clubs like Chelsea because Chelsea were getting all the best youngsters. They had a chief scout who said to the parents "I can do this, I can do that." I coached Terry Venables at Upton Park at night and all of a sudden Terry Venables disappeared and went to Chelsea. Why should kids from Barking or Dagenham go off to Chelsea, not to West Ham?

'Ted Fenton had been a centre half, a charming type of man. I think he was wise enough to realise when he took over as manager at West Ham [in 1950] that the club needed youth and it needed a different outlook. Malcolm Allison came from Charlton for about £6,000 in 1951 and, to me, he was the one who changed West Ham in a considerable way. Malcolm was very enthusiastic, he wanted to get somewhere. Before the Allison era, they were a team known to win at home but not to win away and a lot of people suggested they were happy and contented in the Second Division. They didn't have ambition. Lovely players, but. . .

'Chief scout Wally St Pier was a nice man; West Ham surrounded themselves with nice people. You can count on one hand the number of people who stepped out of line in a major way, and when you reflect on the quality of those who spent their careers there it was an incredible little club. In the 1950s you had Frank O'Farrell, Jimmy Andrews, Dave Sexton, Ernie Gregory, and a fine, upstanding character associated with the club for 50 years, the late Dick Walker. It was a club which didn't seem to have many problem people around. Nice people meet nice people. Eddie Chapman, the secretary, was charming. The youngsters grew up as babies there.

'I don't know whether it was Ted Fenton or Malcolm who had the idea of inviting local youngsters up to the ground on Tuesdays and Thursdays. Perhaps Fenton didn't want to do it himself because he worked with footballers all day, but anyway he chose Malcolm as the guy to do this coaching. I took over from Malcolm and for that duty I received 35 bob a week [£1.75], the standard FA fee. I took the Moores and Hursts.

Depending on conditions, we trained under the stand or we'd go out on the track round the pitch. Occasionally we might be allowed on to the pitch to do a bit of work there. Naturally, it was the highlight for the youngsters if we could. We had a groundsman called George who'd give me a right telling off the following day or even go to Fenton and complain.

'Malcolm took things into his own hands and the groundsman had to grin and bear it. He knew you couldn't make footballers by running around the track. Malcolm wanted to show he had the ability to improve the players – so that was his attitude. If Malcolm thought something was right or there was something we should do, we did it. His influence on the club and me and Bobby was powerful.

'My first recollection of Bobby was that he was a very quiet, modest young man. I think Bobby came to mingle with the senior players like Malcolm and myself and felt it was a privilege just to be there. He took notice of everything, sussed out who he wanted to talk to about the game. He lived quite near Malcolm, so sometimes they travelled on the bus together in the morning.

'Malcolm took me under his wing. And, as I was so close to him, I got close to Bobby. He'd join us in the cafe on the Barking Road near the ground, a real cafe, door-steps of bread and butter. We'd sit round the table – people like [Dave] Sexton and [Frank] O'Farrell would be there – and discuss football. We spent hours and hours there every day. Ted Fenton did a deal with the cafe and gave us vouchers! Eventually, the owner decided we were so many and we spent so much time there that no other customers could get in for lunch so he pushed us upstairs. There would be 15 or 20 of us. People talk about the West Ham Academy. It was there! That would have been the first introduction Bobby had to the Academy. He'd join us and be a quiet listener, listening and having a good time.

'I am sure nothing but football was ever discussed over those lunches and now and again we'd go back to train in the afternoon, still under Malcolm's influence, and try to put into practice the things we had discussed. We didn't have other jobs, other interests.

Fenton would decide after three months' hard slog to give us a day off. He'd take us to Hainault Golf Club, a municipal course; we'd hire four or five clubs and play in our track suits and shoes and that would be it. That was the era when Bobby was a youngster.

'On those afternoons when we decided to go back to train after leaving the cafe, Bobby was always there. I don't think I ever knew him to be late for training or to miss a session. It never crossed my mind to wonder if he was there because he automatically would be. I noticed something else: he was immaculate even when so young, his training gear was always spotless. I know he became famous for being immaculate later on, but he started like that.

'He surrounded himself with people he respected in the game. Like Geoff Hurst, he was a fairly ordinary young player. Being outstanding at school – well schoolboys are schoolboys. We had an exciting one during Bobby's time called Georgie Fenn who scored about a hundred goals for his school, came in with the likes of Moore and got swallowed up. And even Moore didn't have the sort of talent that George Best had at the same age. But soon you could see this lad was going to grow up and be a great player.'

Interestingly, Fenton invited a noted local journalist, Trevor Smith, to have a look at one of Moore's first games for the youth team and Smith remembers a pudgy lad who left no great impression on him.

He didn't take long to leave impressions. By a happy coincidence Dennis Allen had joined Charlton and played against Moore in youth matches. 'He'd grown bigger, taller, stronger, he wasn't a boy any more and, as a player, he was head and shoulders above everyone else. The Charlton–West Ham matches? Well, no prisoners were taken, but he'd smile and laugh and play and he was too good for everybody. Funnily enough, I played centre forward and he marked me. The results went their way because they had a good youth team. He read you and your game all the time. You'd try to put him under pressure, harass him, but you couldn't do it. He was a bit special …'

The reasoning player had been born. Moore lacked pace, an eternal topic of conversation that has woven itself into the folklore of the game. 'This was something he had to think about,' Cantwell says. 'No matter how much training you do, or how much work you do at trying to become quicker, you can't. You can get quicker out of the starting blocks, but if you're not born with speed that's about it. So what he decided to do was to train his mind to be quicker than everybody else's. Before the ball came to him, he decided to know exactly where everyone was positioned on the pitch. He did all his looking before he got the ball, which is an unusual quality in a young player.'

It was this ability which put him in such good stead on that July day in 1966 when the world surrendered. While Nobby Stiles urged Moore to kick the ball over the stand to keep the West Germans at bay, he knew where Hurst was …

Cantwell does remember 'him sitting in the car with me when he was young. You've to be careful what you say to young people and young players, make sure you don't destroy them. He was always a searcher, always asking questions, always asking and not making too many comments himself. So we sat in this car, the first one I ever bought, and he asked me about not having pace. He wanted to know if a footballer could become great without it. Now if I'd said to him that you can't, it would have affected him terribly. He could have said: "There's my ambition gone." I considered my reply and I remember thinking about Johnny Haynes, who we all had the greatest respect for, including Bobby. I told him how Haynes had an ability to get a picture in his mind and see things before the ball ever came to him. People thought Haynes really did have eyes in the back of his head!

'He was able to find space and he knew where all the players – particularly the forwards – were. So, when the ball did come, he put his foot on it and passed it immediately. He didn't put his foot on it then look. He already held the mental picture. I told Bobby to go and watch Johnny Haynes and he'd understand. "Milk turns quicker than him but that doesn't

The 17-year-old Bobby goes off for his first away match after just five days as a League half back in November 1958. Goalkeeper Ernie Gregory shares the train ride to Nottingham.

matter." I could see this cheered him up. And it has been proved that other players made it like that – Pat Crerand, Jim Baxter and Johnny Giles – they weren't pacey.'

Moore made his debut for the England Youth team against Holland in the Olympic Stadium, Amsterdam on 2 October 1957. A player called David Wright of Barnsley captained the side (who was he and where is he now?), but before Moore went off to join the side Allison had a potent chat, telling him that he must captain it. Moore naturally protested that Wright was the captain, but Allison didn't mean that. He instructed Moore to assume the 'role of captain' from centre half, so as to shape and influence and dominate all around him.

Barry Bridges, later famous but at this stage in the Chelsea Youth team, played in that side which travelled to Amsterdam. 'In fact, we played a lot of matches. They seemed to come at you every two or three weeks. I'd get ribbed by the club. They'd say: "What are you, a Chelsea player or an England player?" Bobby was the same then as people would later come to know him. He had an air of control and genuine class both on and off the field – a leader and born to be that. I don't know if he had a nerve in his body or whether he was clever in hiding any insecurity which may have been there. I never really knew him well enough to judge that.

'Before a match at international youth level it could be very tense, and the Olympic Stadium was quite something for teenagers, but he kept perfect self-control and simply carried that out on to the pitch.'

England won that game 3–2. It was the first of Moore's 17 caps in the season of 1957/8. His second cap came against Belgium at Hillsborough where England won 2–0. England were not a bad side, thanks to the coaching of Ron Greenwood, the manager, who described Moore as being 'thirsty for knowledge'.

Moore's 17 caps included the European Championships in Luxembourg, where England lost in the final 1–0 to Italy, and victory in the British Championships – a competition at this and senior level which fashioned the traditional end to each season. England achieved the title by hammering Wales 8–2. Moore captained England Youth at least three times – the records are understandably hazy. So – forgive him – is Barry Bridges, who simply can't remember most of those he played alongside. They are the ones who didn't make it, the ones who departed the stage leaving no impression.

To emphasise this, and thus emphasise what Moore was already achieving, David Barber, the FA's excellent historian who provided much background for this section of the book, could find only a handful of other players he'd heard of among the teams of the time. They included Willie Carlin, who played at Derby County under Brian Clough, Bridges and David Gaskell, who enjoyed a long career in the Manchester United goal.

Bill Rush, a referee in the South East Counties League, was linesman when England Youth played Austria that season. 'People talk about how well Moore read the game, but what struck me then was something else – how well he timed his tackle. I only ever saw one other player as good as Moore at that age, George Burley of Ipswich who went on to play for Scotland.

'After the Austria match we all went to a banquet at a hotel in Lancaster Gate and it didn't finish until around one in the morning. Obviously, the players had a problem getting home so I took some, Bobby and Barry Bridges among them, and dropped them off where they lived. They were strong, fit young men but just a nice bunch.

'I refereed Bobby when he played for West Ham in the Metropolitan League and he was a dream, never a moment's trouble. I think he was only sent off once in all his years at West Ham. All the good things you read about him are true because it's really the way he was.'

Bridges savoured competing against Moore as well as with him: 'He gave you a chance to play because you had in your thoughts his lack of speed.' No doubt Bridges, like a generation to come all over the world, played into the illusion – Moore didn't seem to be there and suddenly was, because he used his brains of course.

Moore played a further match for the England Youth side in season 1958/9 in which they beat Spain 4–2 in Spain and his final record was: played 18, won 12, drawn 2, lost 4.

Doris Frome, who journeyed across Waverley Gardens in April 1941 to see how Mrs Moore and her baby were doing, provides a telling anecdote about the maturing Moore and family discipline. 'He was always in bed before ten, even when he was 17 and at West Ham. His mother would call him in and Robert would go at once.'

Cantwell guards precious memories of Moore's parents. 'They were lovely people. I've an idea his father worked at Ford's at Dagenham. His mother was a big influence, a good-looking woman who Bobby adored and who adored him. Being an only child, they were very protective of him but they didn't interfere. His father was quiet and, as parents, they came and watched him play but I never heard his father raise his voice. I never heard him say the things some fathers do – "Why isn't my son doing this, why isn't the club doing that?" They let West Ham shape Bobby's career.'

Two striking events were taking place in the background of Moore's life, but very much in the foreground at West Ham. In November 1957, Allison was diagnosed as having tuberculosis and missed the rest of the season; in April 1958, West Ham won promotion to the First Division. Allison, Cantwell remembers, 'had been ill and came back and trained like nobody has ever trained on every aspect of his game and played in the reserves in a centre back position.' Thus arose within weeks of West Ham's first season back in the First Division a dilemma, the resolution of which remains momentous and was accompanied at the time by a measure of acrimony.

West Ham opened the 1958/9 season away to Portsmouth, where they won 2–1, and then played Wolves at home. Surely Moore watched this match, drank deep of it, his very own club in the big league and at Upton Park. A crowd of 37,500 delighted as the Hammers beat Billy Wright's side 2–0.

In September, Manchester United were due and wherever they went, great undercurrents of emotion followed. This was the side being reconstructed after the Munich air crash of 6 February 1958 which affected all of Britain and millions beyond who had thrilled to the Busby Babes. No match against Manchester United is an ordinary one, but those played in the aftermath of that tragedy exist in a realm beyond sport altogether.

Of more mundane concern to West Ham, coming to the match, Billy Landsdowne and Andy Nelson were injured, requiring a half-back replacement. As Cantwell remembers: 'Malcolm was my great friend, the closest friend I ever had in football. He shaped my career and shaped Bobby's career and I'd die for him. I'd seen Bobby play in the reserves. I'd trained with him every day and I liked him as a person.

'The day before we played Manchester United, Ted Fenton called me into his office. "I just want to pick your brains," he said. "Left half – what would you do?" I had to think what the choices were, although I knew which players we had. I thought for a while and my choice lay between Malcom and this young lad Bobby Moore – and Malcolm was my dearest friend. I pondered Manchester United and they had a talented but slow player, Ernie Taylor, who'd gone to Old Trafford from Blackpool after the crash. So I told Fenton that I would play Bobby Moore. He looked at me in a sort of amazement. He must have been sure I'd plump for Malcolm because he knew how close we were. I explained: "I'd play Bobby Moore. He's only young but he won't let us down." Fenton agreed and the team sheet went up. Malcolm was absolutely stunned and bitterly disappointed.'

Every inch the model pro ... Bobby at 18.

Although Cantwell remains sure Moore played well and 'we were all very happy', during long tracts of the game Moore appeared frankly unsure of himself. Jeff Ives, now a *Daily Express* sub-editor, watched the match and says: 'Moore was booed because he kept passing the ball back to the goalkeeper. He didn't seem confident enough to do anything else with it.' One should not read too much into this, however tempting it might be to do so, but something can be understood. He was 17 and had reached this debut very quickly and he'd taken Allison's place – the very man who had worked so hard to lift the whole club into the First Division but who was now destined never to play for it there. He had been seen as a venerated, admired, awe-inspiring visionary since his arrival at the club in 1951.

The real point of Moore passing back is that, whatever the crowd wanted, it was safe to do that. He didn't panic and over-reach himself, with the booing rising all around him, nor did he risk doing what he might not be able to do to prove he was a first-team player. Instead, he passed back. As with so much we've already seen, the importance grows retrospectively.

Meanwhile, word had leaked from Ted Fenton's office about Cantwell's advice. He remembers: 'Malcolm got to hear what had happened. Bobby and I and the rest of the team were sitting in the bath after the game, elated. Malcolm came in and glared at me, which he had never done before, and said "Thank you very much. I could have played against Ernie Taylor with my ankles tied together." I felt terrible. Months afterwards, Malcolm said: "Look, you made the correct decision".'

He was right.

PART TWO

BOBBY MOORE

THE PLAYER

BY STEVE CURRY

CHAPTER THREE

WEST HAM AND THE FIRST TRIPS TO WEMBLEY

I t started on a recreation ground in East London where, for generations, young boys have carried their hope on to windswept pitches; the hope that one day one of the touchline figures muffled against the cold will be a scout.

Bobby Moore was no different from the rest.

His opportunity came on a winter's day in 1955 when West Ham manager Ted Fenton dispatched the trusted and vastly experienced Jack Turner to cast an eye over a young player called Moore who had been recommended to the club. It was nothing more than a routine check on the local rec. For Moore, though, it was to be a pivotal moment in his life – his first big match in a journey of heady delights and some bitter disappointments that was to climax with the walk up the most famous staircase in football to collect the game's most coveted prize.

You would not have convinced Turner of that fact back on that cold winter's day. The match was a cup tie between a team of Leyton and East Ham boys and finished in a 3–3 draw. For 15-year-old Moore, it had been neither a particularly distinguished nor disappointing performance. And that was how it was reflected in the handwritten report that Turner submitted to the club's chief scout Wally St Pier.

The report began: 'While he would not set the world alight, this boy certainly impressed me with his tenacity and industry …'

Nothing there to get excited about, yet Turner's intuition made him return for the replay in which Moore scored the winning goal. The rest, you might say, is history and the bond forged with Turner on those open pitches was to develop over the years and spread into a partnership that endured throughout Moore's playing career.

Moore's own recall of his early ambitions went back to when he was 12 and had lost a local cup final 3–1. It was a tearful journey home to his parents because of the awful adolescent belief that the ambition to play football for England, nursed even at primary school, would not now be fulfilled. But this defeat was not the end of his career, and it was only three years later that the local boy received an invitation to train at Upton Park.

Yet, still, the feeling that he was out of place persisted with the young Moore as he looked at a dozen other groundstaff boys whose pedigree seemed so much more impressive. They had played either for Essex or London Schoolboys and many had been trialists with England Schoolboys, while the lad from Barking had made only his district team.

It was this early sense of insecurity that was to be the motivating force which drove Moore to work harder and harder in his single-minded determination to make a successful career out of the game he loved. He was thirsty for knowledge and studied the men who were his idols, Johnny Haynes, Duncan Edwards – whose own life was to be cruelly curtailed at an even younger age – and, less obviously, West Brom's Ray Barlow.

Moore played truant to watch Edwards in the pre-Munich Manchester United at White Hart Lane and yearned for the kind of composure he witnessed as the sturdy young oak from Old Trafford put two goals past Spurs. Among the tears that flowed the day the United plane plunged into the snow were a few of Moore's, for it signalled the passing of a group of genuine schoolboy heroes.

In those days, after becoming a £6 15s 0d (£6.75) groundstaff boy, there was time to study the big names as you swept the terraces and stands of Upton Park. You were as much an odd-job man as a footballer and the glamour was a distant dream for Moore as he helped the other boys pull a heavy roller across the infamously cloying, muddy pitch.

Pitch-rolling was a Friday chore that left the starry-eyed teenagers physically shattered, but that was forgotten the next day as they took their weekly treat of a youth team game. Shortly after his 17th birthday in April 1958, Moore was offered his first professional contract for £12 a week, the maximum salary of the day.

Moore's development was progressing steadily and the boy who had been unable to make it in the Essex Schoolboy team was, at 16, recruited by England at youth level. There, he came under the charge of Ron Greenwood, then assistant manager at Arsenal.

It completed a highly influential double. At club level, the inventive and adventurous wing half Malcolm Allison had made it his business to tutor Moore. Now Greenwood took on his international development. Between them, they represented two of the most respected coaching authorities of their generation.

Moore responded to their precise probing, encouragement and insistence on excellence with rapt attention. Greenwood's philosophies had been moulded by the great Hungarian sides of the early 1950s, and he was anxious to impart his belief in their progressive ideas to the pick of the country's young players. Under Greenwood's direction, Moore's representative career began with a creditable 3–2 win against Holland in the Olympic Stadium in Amsterdam. It was his first visit to one of the major stadia of the world and there would be many more in the years that followed.

The contact with Greenwood at that tender stage was crucial, for it was the beginning of a relationship that coloured Moore's footballing life. It was a coach–player association that was as turbulent and as tempestuous as any marriage between people with firm ideals. They forged between them a mutual respect over football matters that never quite developed into deep friendship.

Moore later recalled that first international: 'I thought I was terrific and I loved Ron for the way in which he had helped me to approach the game.' So great was his respect that Moore slipped alongside Greenwood on the homeward plane and cross-examined him about his beliefs and ideals. 'I was like a puppy dog who followed him around and all the time I was picking his brains,' said Moore. His appetite for knowledge continued as Greenwood coached the England Under-23 side and then arrived at West Ham to replace Ted Fenton in 1961.

Indeed, one of the greatest compliments paid to Moore came when Greenwood told him that his decision to take the manager's job at Upton Park hinged on his belief that he could build a team around Moore. That was how it turned out, their future disputes centring on contracts rather than any conflict on the playing pitch.

Moore was 17 when he discovered that the roar of the crowd was his narcotic and, if the first few steps up the ladder to success had been taken falteringly, there was a sudden spurt from the young defender when he sensed the last few rungs could be attained quickly. Yet his West Ham United debut was always remembered with just a tinge of sadness and regret, for in attaining it he had to leapfrog one of the people to whom he owed most.

There was a straight selection choice for Ted Fenton between the blossoming Bobby and his mentor Malcolm Allison, who had taught Moore so much and who himself was fighting a personal battle against the ravages of tuberculosis. West Ham had been promoted to the First Division in the summer of 1958 and Allison saw a First Division place as an indication that he had finally triumphed over his debilitating illness. Moore, a professional for less than three months and yet to play for the first team, knew what playing against Manchester United that autumn evening would mean to Allison. It was inevitable that Moore's name would eventually replace that of Allison on the team sheet, but it was a bitter blow to him that Moore should do so before his First Division debut for West Ham. However, it was a mark of the man that the first to congratulate Moore on his debut should be the one whose dreams he had shattered.

It was equally poignant, then, that as Moore's life ebbed away after his own fight against illness, Allison should be making one last stand as a football club manager at Bristol Rovers. The news of Moore's death hurt him far more savagely than did the team sheet that night on 8 September 1958 at West Ham when Manchester United were beaten 3–2 and Fleet Street recorded the first commanding steps of Bobby Moore on the road to international stardom.

Moore's memory of that game, as it was of so many he coloured with his style and command, always remained sketchy. 'I hit a couple of balls straight. Nothing really,' he was to recall years later with his usual masterful understatement, though his initial impact was not great. But he remembered more the advice of Allison to be in control of himself, to think big, to look big and to be the director of operations.

Of the torrent of advice imparted by Allison in those early years one sentence was to stand Moore in better stead than the rest. It was: 'Always ask yourself if I get the ball now who do I give it to?' It was, perhaps, the simplest of instructions yet it was to be the cornerstone of Moore's playing strategy, the one that always seemed to enable him to be one moment ahead of all his opponents and which, simply, made him a player with a reputation of having extra-sensory anticipation. The word used in the broader sense for this most useful of facilities would be 'vision'. And Moore not only used it fully himself, he imparted it to younger players as his own experience grew.

He would always know in his own mind who was free to receive a pass and would elaborate: 'There is nothing complicated about vision. It is only the pictures in your mind placed there by looking around yourself. It is so simple. The bad players were those who made the game difficult.' That was never to be an accusation levelled against Moore, whose football, even when the battle was at its fiercest, had about it the calm and serenity of a man fishing in solitude on some faraway river bank.

Yet there were to be salutory lessons for the young Moore and the first one came just three days after that heady debut and the headlines that accompanied it. Moore went to Nottingham Forest for his second match believing that first-team football was a piece of cake. But it was a slice that crumbled very publicly as Johnny Quigley, a wee Scot, ran him ragged as the Hammers plunged to a 4–0 defeat and Moore sought a hole in which to jump. By pure coincidence it was the night of his first date with Tina, who was to be his first wife, and he spent it wondering whether he would ever play again for West Ham. That season, he hardly did.

It was the transfer of John Smith from East to North London in 1960 to join Blanchflower, Mackay and the illustrious company at Tottenham that allowed the gateway to first-team football to crack open again for Moore. He had been growing ever more frustrated at the lack of opportunities, and even when consistent selection came, success did not follow immediately. It was a season of defeats that were often crushing, occasionally humiliating, where West Ham resorted to hitting the kind of long balls that were a betrayal of their established traditions. Moore didn't go much for that and it led to a scepticism about certain management styles that was to stay with him throughout his playing career.

The arrival of Greenwood at West Ham in 1961 was the start of a decade that brought Moore outstanding success at both club and international level and the game's most

The young Bobby Moore practises his skills on the notoriously muddy Upton Park pitch.

Bobby Moore shows off some of West Ham's silverware to an admiring audience. *(Hulton Deutsch)*

Hat-trick hero Geoff Hurst attacks the German goal during the World Cup final of 1966.
(Hulton Deutsch)

It was a rare forward who could get past Moore and take a shot at goal. (*Hulton Deutsch*)

This time the German keeper Tilkowski was able to get a hand to the ball, but he was beaten four times in all. (*Hulton Deutsch*)

(Left) Bobby Moore is carried shoulder high by his triumphant teammates after winning the World Cup. *(Syndication International)*

(Below left) The West Ham connection celebrates England's World Cup victory. From the left: Moore, Geoff Hurst (with trophy) and Martin Peters. *(Varley Picture Agency)*

(Right) The two ambassadors of English soccer – Moore and Charlton – line up on opposite sides in 1967. *(Syndication International)*

(Below) Bobby Moore slides in for another perfect tackle to deny Bobby Charlton. *(Syndication International)*

The complete captain. Moore, in 1967, at the height of his powers. *(Allsport)*

(Right) Pelé and Moore exchange shirts and affection after one of the greatest games of all time between England and Brazil in the World Cup finals of 1970. Moore later called it his finest performance. *(Syndication International)*

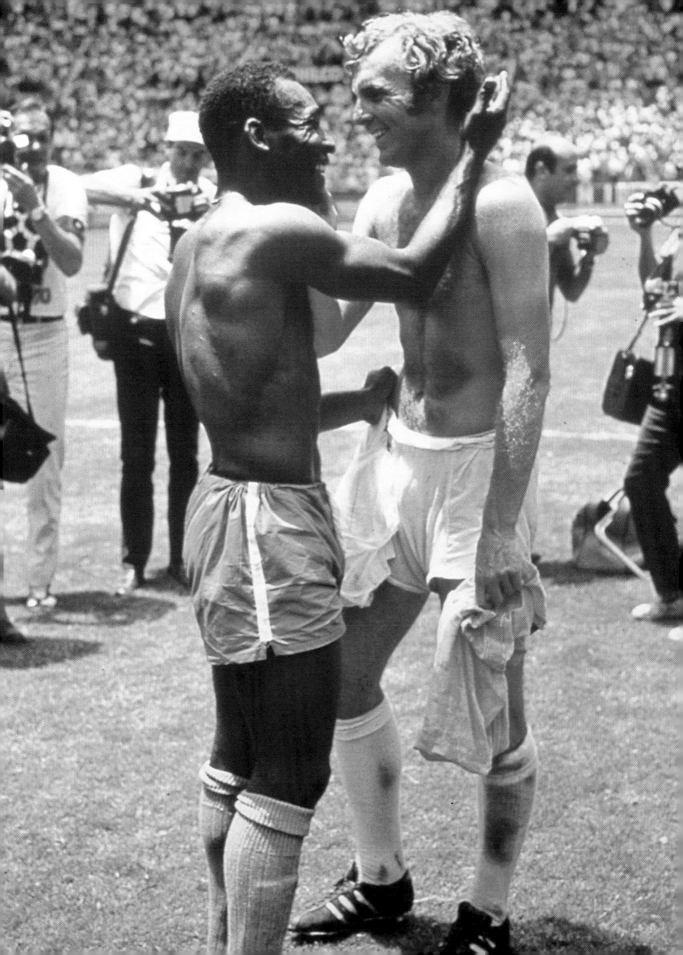

His most bitter disappointment. Moore leads out England for the ill-fated World Cup quarter-final with West Germany at Leon, Mexico, in 1970. England lost 3–2 after leading 2–0 and relinquished the Jules Rimet Trophy. *(Varley Picture Agency)*

The golden boy relaxes after training with England. *(Action Images)*

(Above) By 1961, under new manager Ron Greenwood, Bobby Moore was firmly established in the West Ham side. *(Sport & General)*

(Below) A rare shot at goal from Moore in 1962 as Fulham's George Cohen slides in for the tackle.

coveted prizes: winner's medals in the FA Cup, the European Cup-Winners' Cup and, ultimately, the World Cup. Yet the relationship between the two men was as smooth as a ride on a fairground roller-coaster. There is nothing in the rule book that says you must have harmonious relationships with your manager, which was fortunate in the case of Moore and Greenwood, for what existed between them was something that went deeper than squabbles over money.

They both recognised that, within the sealed-off area of a football pitch, they had a talent that transcended other differences – one was a master coach and the other was a player capable of giving vibrant life to those high ideals. Greenwood was the master of strategy and had at his disposal, in Moore and inside forward Johnny Byrne, the players to apply it both for West Ham and for England in the Under-23 side.

The young captain leads out the Hammers. (*Colorsport*)

Moore always believed those Greenwood talents should have been rewarded with the post of England manager much earlier than his appointment in 1977 in the wake of Don Revie's defection to the Middle East. He knew that the most fitting arena for his encyclopaedic knowledge of the game was at a higher plane than club football. (By the time Greenwood was eventually invited to take the job in his later years, some of his enthusiasm had waned and he viewed it as much as a duty as the challenge it would have been earlier in his career.)

So it was that Greenwood's learned team discussions down at the old Boleyn ground would sound like sheer commonsense to Moore, even if they passed over the head of some of his teammates. But there, more or less, their compatability ended. There was in Greenwood's northern upbringing a quality of restraint and discipline that didn't always match Moore's professional life.

Bobby Moore gets ready for season 1962/3. (*Colorsport*)

Team spirit to the West Ham lads of the early 1960s occasionally involved spirit of a more liquid kind. Moore's liking for lager was enthusiastic, coupled with his evergreen comment that a car needs petrol. It very rarely detrimentally affected his performance even if, on one famous occasion at Blackpool in 1971, it did lead to

Moore and West Ham inside forward Johnny Byrne plot their next moves on the eve of the FA Cup sixth round match with Burnley. They won 3–2 after trailing 2–0.

Moore on tour in America with West Ham in 1963 with manager Ron Greenwood and Johnny Byrne.

Moore goes ten-pin bowling before West Ham's FA Cup fifth round tie with Swindon in 1964.

his being publicly disgraced by Greenwood.

West Ham in the 1960s were synonymous with good football and rich entertainment, and in the season of 1963/4 those factors conspired to provide the team with an FA Cup run which was to end in triumph at Wembley. Their passage through the early rounds was not distinguished. First Charlton were beaten and then, after a replay, Orient were dispatched. Swindon and Burnley followed as the campaign gained momentum and suddenly a semi-final against Manchester United loomed at Hillsborough.

It was to be a huge day for West Ham, crowned by a performance that Moore came to regard as the most outstanding in the club's history. Manchester United were everyone's favourites, with names that tripped off the tongue: Charlton, Law, Best, Crerand.

West Ham, mid-table, were the lambs being led to the slaughter. But on a rain-soaked Yorkshire afternoon they triumphed 3–1 and Moore had taken a gigantic leap towards

announcing himself not only as a fine player but as a leader. Moore recalled that he never saw his manager quite as emotional again as he was on the train journey home from Sheffield. He wept, his head slumped on the table of the dining car and he wanted rid of the fans surrounding his players. The players, wallowing in their achievement, could not and would not understand.

A few weeks later, the Football Writers' Association named him their Player of the Year, an annual award which is still regarded as the domestic game's greatest individual accolade. He was following the steps of some of the greatest names in the game at a glittering dinner traditionally held on the Thursday before the FA Cup final. Moore, at 23, was the youngest-ever recipient.

Just as getting to Wembley was a moment of pride for Moore so the collection of the FWA award was a highlight in his young career. It rankled with him for years afterwards that no one from West Ham United was there to support him that night; the other players had been forbidden to attend and the manager and directors elected not to do so. It was a snub that took some of the satisfaction from the victory that followed 48 hours later when West Ham beat Preston North End 3–2 with goals by Geoff Hurst, John Sissons and Ronnie Boyce. In the moment of victory, however, Moore's efforts to give Greenwood a cuddle were rebuffed.

The 23-year-old Moore proudly displays the Footballer of the Year trophy.

West Ham were heavily backed by the gambling fraternity of East London to win the 1964 final. Preston prepared for the match in the Oatlands Park, a temperance hotel run by the Quakers in the stockbroker belt of Surrey.

All week the discussion surrounded the probability that Preston would field the youngest player to participate in the FA Cup final: Howard Kendall, still 20 days short of his 18th birthday. However, West Ham's John Sissons was only 20 and Ronnie Boyce 21.

It was not a vintage West Ham performance. Second Division Preston took the lead and it was Hammers' resilience more than their skill which turned the game round. Perhaps the semi-final against Manchester United, the impact of that unexpected victory and the anti-climax of facing a Second Division team had robbed them of their bounce.

From the first minutes it seemed West Ham were more affected by nerves than their Lancashire opponents and in the ninth minute Preston went ahead. Doug Holden, a veteran of the Stanley Matthews final of 1953 when he played in Bolton's losing side, slid home a loose ball home after Jim Standen could only block a fine shot from Preston's Alex Dawson. The goal silenced the huge bank of West Ham supporters who strongly out-numbered the visitors from the north.

It was a measure of Moore's cool assurance that West Ham equalised almost immediately, with the skipper instigating the move. He fed the young Sissons who took a return ball from Johnny Byrne to place an angled shot across Preston's Republic of Ireland

West Ham and Preston North End come out on to the famous turf at Wembley in 1964 – although Moore looks calm, it was some time before his side settled down. (*Colorsport*)

Action from the final. (Color-sport)

international goalkeeper Alan Kelly. Moore had shown a captain's mettle and Preston's lapse in concentration had been punished.

Preston, painstakingly prepared by Jim Milne, father of Gordon Milne of Liverpool and England, refused to surrender and, six minutes from half-time, went ahead again with the most memorable of goals from former Manchester United star Dawson, whose reputation flourished at Old Trafford in the wake of the Munich air crash and who had been to Wembley as a teenager in 1958 when United were beaten 2–0 by Nat Lofthouse's Bolton.

Dawson's header, from Davie Wilson's corner, was reminiscent of the great centre forwards like Lofthouse, Dixie Dean, Stan Mortensen and Tommy Lawton. It was a half-time lead that Preston deserved and Ron Greenwood used the short break to jolt West Ham from their inertia, telling them they were looking second best to a team from a lower division. Eddie Bovington was detailed to curtail the damage being done by Alan Spavin while Boyce was told to sit tighter on Nobby Lawton.

The reorganisation stemmed Preston's flow and in the 53rd minute Moore's side drew level again. It was a fortunate equaliser. Peter Brabrook's corner was turned goalwards by Geoff Hurst. Kelly touched the ball on to his crossbar, but as it came down it hit the luckless Preston keeper and crossed the line. For the second time in the match, Hammers had come back from behind and their confidence lifted. Brabrook and Sissons created problems on the wings, but Hurst and Byrne squandered the chances and it seemed that Preston might take the match into extra time.

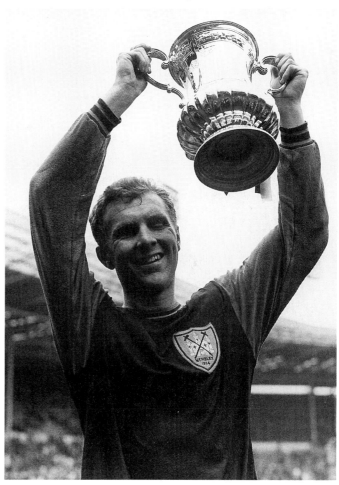

Moore holds aloft his first major trophy after West Ham had beaten Preston 3–2 in the 1964 FA Cup final. *(Sport & General)*

Then, with injury time being played, West Ham got their winner. Hurst and Brabrook created the opening against a physically shattered side and Brabrook provided the final centre for Boyce to head the winner. And so it was Bobby Moore who went up to collect the FA Cup at the age of 23.

Many players go to Wembley in an FA Cup final and emerge, whether with a winner's or loser's medal, deflated by the experience. Moore always remembered the game as an anti-climax. He said later: 'We had been so good in the semi-final that Wembley that day should really have belonged to West Ham. It was good to win the first major honour but

'It's all mine,' says a beaming Bobby. (*Colorsport*)

apart from that it was a wash-out. As a team we just never played well.'

The victory banquet may have carried the atmosphere of a wake rather than a celebration for Moore, but the success opened the door to European competition where Greenwood's coaching ability found its full range.

At the start of the next season Greenwood nursed the firm belief that his side could win the League Championship. They had beaten the bigger teams in their Cup final year and lost to the less fashionable ones. But the loss of Moore with a groin injury at the end of October 1964 proved a severe blow – even though his absence gave the public a first glimpse of a man who was to share later glories with his club skipper, Martin Peters.

Greenwood prepared his players for their European experience by sending them

Moore outside West Ham in 1964 during the first of several contract disputes with the club. It was a controversial start to their glorious Cup-Winners' Cup season.

We've won the Cup!
Moore holds the FA Cup
after the 3–2 defeat of
Preston in the 1964
final.

abroad on scouting missions to watch the opposition play in Sunday games. Some of it must have worked, for West Ham went through the first round 2–1 on aggregate against La Gantoise of Belgium.

West Ham, minus Moore, beat Spartak Sokolov 3–2 on aggregate. Against Lausanne, with Moore now back in the side, the margin was slightly more encouraging, with a 2–1 away win followed by a 4–3 thriller at Upton Park in which Brian Dear made his impact with two important goals.

Real Zaragoza of Spain were tough semi-final opponents, but in the first leg at Upton Park West Ham coasted to a two-goal lead with goals from Dear and Byrne within 24 minutes. Zaragoza pulled one back to leave the tie finely balanced for the second leg in northern Spain. Greenwood was worried about the loss of the injured Byrne for the second game, but he knew that Moore would provide the stabilising influence.

Laperta scored after 23 minutes for the Spaniards to level the aggregate, before the maturing Sissons made it 1–1 just before half-time. The second half belonged to Moore as

West Ham held on to reach the final against the German side TSV Munich 1860.

For a club that had enjoyed little success over the years, the place in the 1965 European Cup-Winners' Cup was a true reward for the loyal fans from East London, especially as Wembley had been pre-selected as the venue.

For Bobby Moore it was the chance to make a quick return to what was becoming his spiritual home and to erase the disappointing performance of 12 months earlier. This West

Moore trains alone as he recovers from the groin strain that kept him out of the early rounds of the 1964/5 Cup-Winners' Cup.

Ham United did with an irresistible performance. The plain statistics show that Hammers won with two second-half goals in the space of three minutes from Alan Sealey, the first an angled shot and the second an easy tap-in from a free-kick taken by Moore.

Moore explained the sophisticated success by the fact that West Ham had got the feel of Wembley from the previous season. 'If winning the World Cup has to be the pinnacle of my career, the game that gave me the most satisfaction at club level was the win over Munich. It was the best of both worlds, playing with your mates, lads you train with week in, week out, and in front of your own fans in a major final on the international stage. Wonderful! Munich weren't mugs because they had beaten Torino in the semi-final and they were the side who were strongly fancied to win the final. They had four internationals, too, and the Yugoslav national goalkeeper. It was a tremendous performance on a marvellous occasion. We had a very talented side, even if it was one

that needed to find real consistency.'

Two finals in the space of a year – and two tropies. The people of East London were ecstatic and they could hardly wait for the start of the following season. But they, like their team, their manager and their captain, were to be bitterly disappointed as the club plummeted into decline.

West Ham were the victims of their own ideals. They delighted in the sweet simplicity of their football, but it also contained a fragility which was to leave them in a permanent spiral as stronger, more aggressive sides came in and kicked the jigsaw to pieces.

The Hammers were getting into the habit of celebrating at Wembley. This time it was the European Cup-Winners' Cup in Moore's hands. (Sport & General)

A triumphant Moore lifts the Cup-Winners' Cup at Wembley in 1965 after the 2–0 defeat of Munich 1860.

Moore spent many years analysing why West Ham never found total fulfilment from the football coached by Greenwood and his assistant John Lyall. The problem was that, while everyone who loved the game wanted to watch football at West Ham, other teams also liked playing there for they knew they would be allowed the space to play themselves. That reputation as a soft touch was to stay with West Ham throughout the 1970s.

For Moore, however, there were diversions. His international career

Moore displays the Cup-Winners' Cup to the fans from the balcony of East Ham Town Hall.

had been steadily and impressively taking shape long before the two Wembley club finals. The coaching of Greenwood through the England youth system and for the Under-23 side had developed Moore's aptitude and appetite for the really big occasions.

Moore had been the industrious young leader of West Ham's side during the 1961/2 season and felt he had earned the enjoyment of a relaxing club summer tour to Nigeria and Rhodesia. So when Greenwood called him into his office and told his 21-year-old

Captain of club and country ... Moore in 1966.

captain he would not be going on the club tour Moore wanted to explode and demanded: 'What have I done wrong?'

His manager's face creased into a smile. 'Walter wants you to go to Chile,' he said. The graduation Moore had hoped for had arrived. Walter Winterbottom, the England manager, had called him into his squad for the 1962 World Cup. Moore deserved the promotion for he had played in the Under-23 sides which had beaten Israel 7–1 at Leeds, gone to Holland and won 5–2, and thrashed Scotland 4–2 at Aberdeen.

Moore had also played for Young England against England on what was then a traditional eve of Cup final game. As had come to be expected, his impact on the game had been considerable. 'The Under-23s always had a good go at the seniors because they were out to make a mark and this match was no different,' he said. 'But none of us imagined for a minute that there were World Cup places at stake. We all believed the squad was already picked.'

In fact it was, more or less. But Greenwood's insistence that Moore was ready for that level of football had swung a late decision. So Moore travelled to South America, but the widespread belief was that he was going simply to gain experience. There was no hint that he was about to be thrown in at the deep end. Moore accepted the selection with his usual calm, but inside the fires were burning. He wanted to play a senior international – and it was to be sooner rather than later.

CHAPTER FOUR

CAPTAIN OF ENGLAND

———————

When Moore climbed aboard a BOAC flight for South America on 17 May 1962, he could have had little idea how the World Cup line-up was formulating in the mind of Walter Winterbottom during the 17-hour journey via New York and Kingston. The manager was wrestling with various team permutations for England's final friendly match against Peru in Lima. Defence was his preoccupation, for Peter Swan, the holder of the centre-half position, was suffering from mild tonsilitis. In any event, speculation was increasing that this berth might go to Tottenham's tall, dark defender Maurice Norman, who had been understudy to Billy Wright in the Sweden World Cup four years previously.

There was no hint to Moore that he would be asked to make his international debut. Following the 1958 Manchester United Munich air disaster, players were invariably divided between two flights. In this instance, the first flight arrived 24 hours before the second and it seemed logical that the team to meet Peru would be together on the first. When Moore was asked to travel on that flight, it crossed his mind that he might be a shock selection. But then Winterbottom switched him to the second plane and he accepted a mistake had been made and he really was just along for the ride.

While the debate over Swan and Norman rumbled on, Winterbottom had the big surprise still in his waistcoat pocket – he was going to give Moore his debut in preference to either Bobby Robson or Stan Anderson, the two players who had hitherto been wrestling for the No. 4 shirt. Both had vastly more experience than Moore, but the 21-year-old West Ham defender was handed the opportunity on the strength of his positive tackling and an ability to defend and attack with almost equal merit. Moreover, Moore, Norman and Blackburn's Bryan Douglas, brought in as replacement for John Connelly, had been given the indication that if they played well in Peru they might be in the team for the first World Cup match.

So it was that on a warm, sultry, Sunday afternoon, thousands of miles from his Barking birthplace, Moore's distinguished international career – the greatest in England's history – was born. And how. He, Norman and Ron Flowers looked a compact half-back line and the result was just about as perfect as England could have wished, a four-goal success with Jimmy Greaves scoring a hat-trick. Moore's own part was to give an assured performance.

He moved into the England training camp in the foothills of the Andes a happy young man looking forward to the preliminary matches against Hungary, Argentina and Bulgaria, even though there was still no real guarantee he would be involved in the games being played in Rancagua. His chances improved, however, when Bobby Robson damaged an ankle in training, thus robbing him of several days of valuable preparation.

The Championships got off to a dreadful start, and after only two days and eight games it was apparent that determination to succeed was swamping any chance of their being remembered for fine play. Violence, ill-temper and serious injury spewed from fiercely unlawful football. In England's group, Argentina's treatment of Bulgaria was particularly brutal. Stud marks were in evidence on most players and two of the Bulgarians were put out of the competition. It was in this climate that England entered their first game against Hungary. Moore was in the side again on what might have been an English winter's day: chilly and wet.

Perhaps England had left some of their enthusiasm and playing strength on the training pitch, for this was a disappointing performance, without either spark or inspiration. They were beaten 2–1. Although Hungary were a more functional side than they had been in the 1950s, they still played neat, passing football and England spent most of the game on the defensive. Moore, charged with marking a long-striding inside forward called Tichy, did that job splendidly, even if some of the link play with Johnny Haynes was sacrificed. There was no way he could be blamed. England were under pressure and he fulfilled his task with merit. So much so that he was selected for the second match against Argentina, the only change in the side being Alan Peacock replacing Gerry Hitchens.

The mood in the England quarters was lifted by an exhilarating 3–1 victory, Flowers converting a penalty and Jimmy Greaves and Bobby Charlton each notching a goal. For Moore, it was an excellent match. He was detailed to mark Sanfilippo, then regarded as one of the world's great ball-players. Moore loved the big occasion, finding it more comfortable than he could have imagined. He enjoyed, particularly, his rapport with Haynes, who he felt was always available to receive the ball.

Sir Stanley Rous, the President of FIFA, felt it was necessary before the third round of the preliminary matches to make an appeal to all 16 competing clubs for a return to sportsmanship, for there had been a match between Chile and Italy in Santiago that had been little short of a pitched battle. England, against Bulgaria, the weakest team in their group, were ready to heed that request, while the East Europeans were looking to salvage at least a point to take home.

Consequently, the match was a desperately boring, goalless draw. Some of the England side were tired and might have been replaced with fresh legs. But, for the young Moore, it was just a dreary game. He recalled it later as perhaps the worst international he played in. 'They had lost their two group matches and we needed a draw to make sure we progressed,' he said. 'They just played us with nine men in their own half. We were trying to play the game, but when we realised what they were up to we were not prepared to take chances either. We would pass the ball around in our half and then knock it forward. They would win it back and do the same. It was terrible, one of the worst internationals of all time.' Both sides were hooted from the pitch by the Chilean crowd who believed that Bulgaria had deliberately allowed England safe passage into the quarter-finals.

England had made it to the last eight and their opponents were Brazil, the 1958 champions and widely tipped to win again. Very much the underdogs, England still approached the game in Vina Del Mar optimistically. Moore certainly believed in the team's chances, but then he had to admit he had never seen the opposition play. It was to his credit that he was regarded as an automatic choice for the game even though it was still only his fourth appearance. The game was to signal England's exit from the competition, although they went out in a manner that brought no disgrace and to a team that was festooned with enough talent to enable them to retain the trophy.

There were some legendary names in the Brazilian side: Garrincha, Vava, Didi, Nilton Santos, Zito, Amarildo and Zagalo. They had experience, too, as many of them had been in the winning side four years earlier. England had Gerry Hitchens in for the injured Peacock and it was felt some of the older Brazilians might feel the physical pressure after such a tight match schedule. Not a bit of it. They used their craft to pace themselves through an exciting and exacting match.

Garrincha, just rising to his peak in this competition, headed the Brazilians into the lead midway through the first half. Few believed England could recover. You could almost sense the relief in the England side when Haynes dropped a free kick into the penalty area, Greaves headed against a post and Hitchens swept home the rebound. Now the fans had a game and England's confidence was rising.

But at the start of the second half, Brazil restored their lead after Flowers conceded a free kick on the edge of the area. Moore recalled later: 'Garrincha suddenly produced one of his famous free kicks. It bent all over the place. I had never seen anything like it and it thumped into Ron Springett's chest and Vava pounced on it.' The Brazilians called it Garrincha's 'dry leaf shot' and Springett would not argue the point for it drifted enough to deceive him.

England had to push forward then and while they were chasing the game Garrincha finished them off, his 25-yard shot arrowing into the top corner of the England net. Moore said: 'It was like eating candy. We didn't stop behind to see them beat Czechoslovakia. I knew they would win it after they had beaten us and they put four past Chile in the semi-final. It seemed they could turn on the magic when they chose to.'

So England went home without the victory they had yearned for and with a manager whose days in charge were numbered as the Football Association at last set about putting the selection of their sides on a more professional footing. Winterbottom was still in charge the next season when Moore, fresh from his honeymoon with Tina, was selected for his home international debut in October 1962 at Sheffield Wednesday's Hillsborough in the European Nations' Cup. England drew disappointingly 1–1 and Moore felt that his emergence in the side was coinciding with the end of an era … and the start of another.

Moore retained affectionate memories of Winterbottom, who had, after all, taken the big gamble with him before the 1962 World Cup, an experience that stood Bobby in excellent stead throughout his playing career. 'As manager he was a warm man who was never happier than when talking about skills, attitudes and tactics. He knew the name of every good player in every country, with their strengths and weaknesses. He was a walking encyclopaedia on football. He had been responsible for getting the coaching organised in this country and at youth level upwards he'd been a great help to me. But the old system of having an FA selection committee made up of amateurs must have been a nightmare for him.'

Captain and manager … Moore and Alf Ramsey in 1965.

He stayed on to negotiate England through an away victory in Ireland, with Mike O'Grady getting a couple of goals, and a 4–0 home win over Wales while his bosses in Lancaster Gate were negotiating terms of reference with Alf Ramsey, who had led Ipswich Town to the First Division Championship. He had specified that he alone would be responsible for the team selection. But his first choices tumbled as disastrously in Paris as if they had been dropped from the top of the Eiffel Tower.

The match in Paris on 27 February 1963 was the start of Alf's long career as England manager that was to embrace the ultimate success. Yet in that first game, all that happened was that Moore had his worries about the state of the team confirmed by a messy, disorganised performance. At half-time Ramsey remained calm as he urged the team to have faith in themselves and their footballing ability.

However, the 5–2 defeat signalled the start of Alf's quiet revolution and he turned to the young Moore to seek answers to the important questions about how things had been done in the past. The West Ham defender from Barking and the manager from Dagenham started their partnership that night on the coach carrying the England players away from the Paris stadium. It was an interesting chemistry between the two Essex men, for neither of them was an emotional person. Alf could seem very detached, though this might have been to cover up possible shyness, but like Moore, he had the cold steel of determination and ambition in his resolve.

It would take time, of course, but things changed. Gordon Banks was introduced in goal to help the defensive organisation. Bobby Charlton was restored on a permanent

basis and George Eastham was drafted into midfield. A 4–2 victory over Czechoslovakia in Bratislava was another highly significant date in the history of Ramsey, Moore and England – and one that was to stay in Moore's memory whenever and wherever he was to pull on the white shirt which he wore with so much pride.

Jimmy Armfield was injured for England's match against Czechoslovakia on 20 May 1963, and Alf Ramsey had no qualms about handing the captaincy to Bobby Moore. It was only his 12th international, but he had shown the qualities of leadership which Ramsey wanted for his side. Moore perhaps felt he was merely fulfilling his football destiny because he admitted later: 'I loved the experience of just leading the team out. I decided that England would lose the match over my dead body. The crowd was noisy and partisan and I knew that we were not meeting a poor team.'

This was the Czechoslovakia of Masopust which had reached the final of the World Cup the previous season. It was another turning point for England in Moore's mind, as Jimmy Greaves scored twice along with the two Bobbys – Smith and Charlton – to provide a resounding 4–2 victory. Victories against East Germany (2–1) and Switzerland (8–1) followed, and Moore had been the only player to take part in every match of that post-1962 World Cup season.

So it continued relentlessly through the 1963/4 season, with Ramsey tinkering to produce an England side of flair, organisation, skill and spirit. A one-goal defeat in Glasgow was the only hiccup, but there were seven victories either side of it. What was significant was that the defeat at Hampden signalled the end of Jimmy Armfield as an automatic choice, though he had enjoyed a brilliant international career and was still to be in the squad for the World Cup in 1966.

While Moore was being established as skipper, Ramsey was running through trials with players in other positions. The summer tour in 1964 was a disappointment. Although England dismissed the USA 10–0 in a match Moore sat out, England went on to lose to Brazil and Argentina and to draw with Portugal in a four-nation tournament in Brazil.

But England were unbeaten in 1964/5 as Moore witnessed an increasing number of Ramsey's experiments. Moore played alongside his old friend Terry Venables in a 2–2 draw against Belgium at Wembley and with his West Ham teammate Johnny Byrne against Scotland – another 2–2 draw in which the striker he so admired received a serious knee injury.

Later, on the summer tour of 1965, a shape began to appear that would serve England so dramatically and successfully in the following season. Ray Wilson, Nobby Stiles, Jack Charlton and Alan Ball, all players who would provide impetus to the World Cup effort, were introduced into Ramsey's equation. It was a successful trip: a draw in Belgrade and victories in West Germany and Sweden.

England scheduled 12 matched for the 1965/6 season as their preparation for hosting the World Cup. While other European and South American sides were engaged in playing qualifying matches, Ramsey was left to find nations willing to keep England in trim for the competition. Austria obliged by coming to Wembley and winning. A match against Poland at Goodison Park on 5 January 1966 provided Moore with the first of only two international goals. Yet Ramsey gave his skipper one more moment of concern in the summer tour that immediately preceded the Word Cup. The squad had been nominated and numbered from 1 to 22. Players were told that these were the numbers they would

keep throughout the competition. Moore was his usual No. 6 and the belief was that the first 11 named would be the most likely starting line-up. However, when the warm-up tour started in Finland, Moore found himself left out of the side. He was naturally concerned. 'There had been a few voices calling for Norman Hunter to be in the side and when they won 3–0 against Finland with Norman involved it made me sit up. From that moment on, I never expected to be selected for England until the letter from the FA dropped through the letter box. I never again took my selection for granted.'

The 1966 World Cup squad gather before the match with Uruguay. Pictured here with Moore are Jimmy Greaves, Geoff Hurst, Ray Wilson, Alan Ball and manager Alf Ramsey.

He needn't have worried, since he was back for the next game in Oslo played in front of the old King of Norway. Moore admitted: 'Nobody was more relieved to see his name on the team sheet than I was.' And nobody was more on their toes. England swept to a 6–1 victory, with Jimmy Greaves grabbing four and Moore kept his place in Copenhagen where he led England to a 2–0 success.

Those who travelled on that tour remember how the England team spirit was building up under the meticulous gaze of Ramsey. He knew he might not have the best players in the World Cup but he was certain they would be the best prepared team. He chose Poland for the final warm-up game because he knew they would jolt the side back to reality after the comparatively easy matches in Scandinavia. Moore gave one of his more majestic performances out in the wilds of Chorzow before a baying, partisan Polish crowd. A goal from Roger Hunt sealed victory and England flew home convinced about their credibility, even invincibility, for the task ahead.

The nation was in a state of high readiness as Ramsey's squad moved into their headquarters at Hendon Hall, almost within hearing distance of the roar of the Wembley crowd. It was in the hotel, with its stately home atmosphere, that one last drama was enacted prior to the first game against Uruguay.

Moore had been the target of several clubs and the possessive Ron Greenwood was equally determined his most prized property should not go on the market. But talks between West Ham's captain and manager regarding a new contract remained unresolved in those early days in July. Under FA rules, that meant Moore did not exist as a player. Hurried talks took place as Greenwood hastened to Hendon and a month's contract to clear the skipper for the World Cup was signed. The crisis was over. But Moore still believed that when the World Cup was finished he might be allowed to sign for Tottenham Hotspur, where he would have joined his friend Terry Venables. That was what Spurs manager Bill Nicholson wanted, too.

CHAPTER FIVE

1966 – THE DREAM COMES TRUE

The Jules Rimet Trophy is made of gold, stands no higher than a beer bottle and weighs 9lb. It is a statue of a winged seraphim and it was, until the Brazilians won it outright in 1970, the most coveted trophy in football. It took the Football Association six years to plan the World Cup and their representatives 19 days to win it. They had, it is true, the advantage of playing all their six matches in the same stadium, which they regarded very much as their home territory. To Bobby Moore it certainly was.

He was always comfortable there. He felt it was a ground befitting his talents. He had played at Wembley for West Ham and won trophies there, and he had developed and honed his international talents on its billiard table surface. The anticipation of the nation was not lost on him. That summer month the rest of the world seemed to stand still. There might have been a financial freeze and, yes, there was growing conflict in the Middle East. But somehow it didn't seem to matter. Even people whose interest in football had always been peripheral now turned to the newspapers, radio and television for every snippet of news concerning the England team.

For Alf Ramsey, who had boldly declared without reservation that 'England will win the World Cup', this was the moment of truth. He said it twice, once to a local journalist in Suffolk and again at a London press conference on 1 May 1963, soon after he took over the England post. For a man not given to controversial outbursts, it was one that was to be thrown back at him so many times before the ultimate triumph. Alf had always carried a chip on his shoulder at not being the first choice for the post of manager. There had been 59 applications when the job was advertised, but the six-man selection committee did not believe a suitable applicant was among them. Jimmy Adamson, the thoughtful Geordie from Burnley FC, was heavily fancied but decided he wanted to carry on playing for a few more years. Winterbottom's own choice would have been Ron Greenwood, but he was not to be given the opportunity until 1977.

Ramsey seemed the right man, an ex-international with 32 caps who had managed Ipswich for seven years and taken them from the Third to First Division and won the Second and First Division titles in successive seasons. As a player at Southampton and Tottenham, Ramsey had been blessed with ability and discipline, plus a notable understanding of the game and an unflappable temperament. They had called him 'The General' as a full back at White Hart Lane. But he was also his own man. He saw something of himself in the young Moore, which persuaded him that here was the player to lead England towards perhaps their best opportunity yet to win the World Cup of the game they had given to the rest of the world.

And so it was that, on 11 July 1966 at Wembley, the Queen, dressed in a green coat and white hat, finally opened the final stages of the World Cup. The combined Guards bands played, local schoolboys decked in the colours of the 16 finalists paraded and Alf fidgeted with his tie.

The match was England v Uruguay, the hosts against the two-time winners who had staged the first World Cup back in 1930. The team selected was very approximate to that which would contest the final, though Greaves was preferred to Hurst and Connelly to Peters. The crowd of 87,000 had paid £68,000 for the privilege of saying they were there. They might have been entitled to ask for their money back.

'We just didn't function at all,' was how Moore summed up the match which fizzled out into a goalless draw. To be fair to England, Uruguay had lacked ambition and Ramsey's men continually ran into areas deeply populated by South American players. The defence played immaculately but had little to threaten them; the midfield worked hard to create the openings. But it was a night of sterility and on the big occasion England found themselves leaving the pitch to hoots of derision, while Uruguay celebrated what they considered a fine result.

The old stadium had lacked emotion on that first big night and Ramsey made a couple of adjustments to his side for the second game against Mexico: Terry Paine replaced John Connelly and Martin Peters came in for Ball. Mexico, too, turned out to be a negative side and, though they were clearly beaten by goals from Bobby Charlton and Roger Hunt, there was still an uneasy feeling that this was not a side with the appearance of potential champions. 'Frankly, we struggled until the moment Bobby Charlton got a goal,' Moore admitted. That goal was a beauty struck with ferocity by Charlton from 30 yards and it somehow lifted the spirits of those close to the England camp.

The third qualifying game was against a French side who were, by general consensus, only ordinary. The fact that England defeated them 2–0, Roger Hunt scoring the goals, did not dispel the foreboding that England might not have the depth of quality to go all the way. Ramsey was alternating his wingers and Moore would reflect: 'Alf was always crucified for not playing with wingers, yet that is what he really wanted to do. He had four in the party but none of them brought us success. So he ended up playing Ball and Peters.'

That was his solution for the quarter-final, where England came up against the talented but temperamental Argentinians, who had won few friends in their qualifying group in the Midlands. For all their skill, they had been in a provocative and petty mood.

It was a nervous build-up. Changes were necessary as Greaves had four stitches in a gash to his shin and that meant a call-up for Geoff Hurst. Greaves was heartbroken and no soothing words from Moore, his roommate at Hendon Hall, could console him. Ball was then promoted above Callaghan for a match where the players sensed there were lurking dangers.

If Argentina had concentrated on playing football, England could have been beaten. Instead, they indulged in every sinister trick in the book. They spat, kicked, argued and pinched. They body-checked, shirt-pulled and play-acted. FIFA's disciplinary body were to put it another way. 'They brought the game into grave disrepute by their flagrant breaches of the laws and disregard for discipline and good order.'

Moore brought restraint to his side, thanks to his own example, urging them to be detached from the trouble; he was determined that England's shape should not be disrupted. However, Argentina's captain, the tall, talented but arrogant Antonio Rattin, was at the heart of his team's tantrums. This was an abuse of a fine talent, for he was an excellent, creative midfield player. But that afternoon something triggered in him a desire to provoke that eventually forced German referee Rudolf Kreitlin to send him off. Ray Wilson sat on the ball while the Argentinians argued and FIFA officials gathered on the touchline.

Rattin went, slowly, reluctantly, and still spouting his indignation. But his parting gave England the shaft of light they had been seeking. Moore believed it was the understanding built at West Ham between Peters and Hurst that did it for England, a near-post cross and a glancing header from Hurst gave them the lead. Certainly, it was the kind of goal seen with great frequency around that time at Upton Park.

Ramsey stoked the fires after the game when he suggested England's best football was still to come. 'It will come against the right type of opposition,' he said. 'A team who come to play football and not act as animals.' It was an expression that was to bring Alf a FIFA rebuke but which, on the evidence of that warm weekend afternoon at Wembley, was not far off the truth.

Moore now had no doubts that England could and would win the trophy and the rest of the country was coming to share his view. Moore was convinced Portugal could not defeat England, that they would make it an occasion but they did not really have the capacity to punish. They had excellent players in the tall Torres and the elusive Simoes. They had Eusebio, too, but Moore felt that he did not fancy coming up against England's toothless tiger, Nobby Stiles.

And so it proved, with Portugal playing some neat and colourful football but without the penetration to unsettle Moore and his organised defence. Portugal did not commit a foul until the 57th minute, which contrasted sharply with their brutal treatment of Pelé when they had played Brazil earlier in the competition. But, by then, Bobby Charlton had put England ahead and he then secured the place in the final with one of his searing long-range shots that set the heart pounding. Eusebio's penalty eight minutes from time came too late. Moore would say: 'For the first time, we felt the crowd were in there with us and thank God we gave them something to cheer about.'

There was barely a soul in England that 30 July who didn't awake to a feeling of excited anticipation. England v West Germany in the World Cup final. It was boom time for the TV rental companies and for anyone else selling anything remotely connected to football.

At Hendon, the England skipper was consoling his friend Greaves, who had been left out of the side. Moore found himself feeling sorry for Greaves yet so happy for his own club colleague Hurst. Wembley was a ground aching with a sense of occasion and in the dressing room there was hardly any space to move, with so many well-wishers and photographers. There was such mayhem that Moore didn't remember the walk up the

England celebrate their 2–1 victory over Portugal in the World Cup semi-finals. Moore embraces Nobby Stiles while Bobby Charlton, Gordon Banks and Roger Hunt get into a huddle.

Relaxing before the World Cup final with Ron Flowers and Jimmy Greaves (seated).

The teams line up before the final – a few players kick a ball around to calm their nerves. *(Hulton Deutsch)*

Referee Gottfried Dienst tosses the coin as Moore and his German counterpart Uwe Seeler look on anxiously. Soviet linesman Tofik Bakhramov, who made one of the most hotly debated decisions in the history of the game, stands next to Seeler. *(Hulton Deutsch)*

tunnel, the hand-shakes or the toss-up.

His mind clicked into gear as the game unfolded, only to be jolted by a German goal. It was Ray Wilson's mistake, a weak, headed clearance, and Helmut Haller drove it past Banks for England to concede their first goal in open play in the tournament. But Moore had not come this far to be beaten. He floated a 35-yard free kick into the penalty area and Hurst had read it perfectly, timed his run and headed inside the right-hand post. It was 1–1.

Then, in the second half, there was elation as Ball's corner was driven at the defence by Hurst, the ball spun into space and Peters pounced. 'At that moment, I thought we had won,' Moore recalled. 'And for the first time I was conscious of the voices singing.'

But the Germans were not finished yet. They won a free kick 10 yards

One of the less memorable moments of the World Cup final as Peters finds himself being entered into referee Dienst's book.
(Hulton Deutsch)

Gordon Banks saves to keep England's hopes alive.
(Hulton Deutsch)

outside the area. Emmerich took it, Moore appealed for handball by Schnellinger but was ignored. Weber rolled the ball home with just a minute to go. The replay showed the foul should have been given the other way, but it was too late.

In the interval before extra time, Alf was composed: 'You have won the World Cup once. Now go and win it again. Look at the Germans. They are flat out. They can't live

with you for another half hour.' Still, the game had one more twist, for as Ball cut inside and delivered the pass, Hurst's shot thumped the underside of the bar and bounced. Was it over the line, or not? Nobody will ever know for sure. It became perhaps the most debated goal in football history. Soviet linesman Tofik Bakhramov had no doubt. Referee Gottfried Dienst conferred with him for what seemed an age before

Martin Peters (No. 16) turns to celebrate after he has scored England's second goal, which seemed to have secured the final for England.
(Hulton Deutsch)

awarding the goal. Moore, 50 yards away, was in no position to judge but felt that it must have crossed the line for Roger Hunt to turn away in celebration when he could have knocked the loose ball over the line.

Moore's arm is raised in an appeal for handball by Schnellinger (immediately in front of him), but Weber's (on the ground) goal stood and extra time beckoned. *(Hulton Deutsch)*

In the end, it didn't matter because England got a fourth. It was fitting that it should be Moore who supplied the pass. Hurst remembers wanting his captain to hump the ball to safety, but that was not Moore's style. Hurst said: 'Bobby had it beautifully under control. I saw him glance up and then I made the gesture that seasons of playing together told him I was ready for the pass. And it came.' Hurst ran on to grab his hat-trick goal as Kenneth Wolstenholme on BBC television uttered those immortal words as the fans came on the pitch. 'They think it's all over,' he said. 'It is now.' And it was. Moore, overwhelmingly voted the player of the tournament, had little recall of those immediate moments when Jack and Bobby Charlton wept openly. He did remember his hands were dirty and that the Queen was wearing white gloves. He wiped them clean on the velvet drape over the Royal Box.

Each time Moore looked at the re-run of those heady ecstatic scenes it sent a shiver down his spine. 'It is the be all and end all,' he said. Moore, the supreme captain, had been there. And done it.

The pride shows in Moore's expression as he holds aloft the famous gold trophy. *(Hulton Deutsch)*

Bobby made sure that he wiped his hands before the greatest moment of his career – he had seen how white the Queen's gloves were and didn't want to dirty them. *(Hulton Deutsch)*

The toothless grin of Nobby Stiles was one of the most enduring images of a day that was so full of great memories. *(Hulton Deutsch)*

As the trophy was passed round the team, the previously tearful Charlton brothers made sure that they were never far away. *(Hulton Deutsch)*

By kissing the Jules Rimet Trophy, Moore finally convinced himself that he was captain of the greatest team in the world. *(Hulton Deutsch)*

CHAPTER SIX

THE COMPLETE PLAYER

There had to be a sense of anti-climax for the England players after their stunning Wembley success. When you have touched the summit of the highest mountain what is there left? Moore went back to West Ham a hero and now an international personality. But on the football field, which was his place of work, it was a matter of maintaining a level of performance. And that was not always easy at a club where ideals remained high but achievements, after the successes of the mid-1960s were to be low.

Moore often reflected on his club career and what he might have achieved had he been able to join any one of the clubs whose interest in him passed down the telephone lines into Upton Park. He also talked to other managers, without any qualms that he might be

betraying West Ham. Managers, he argued, did their own negotiations – why not players? But the one career move he felt he wanted to take was to join Brian Clough. The two men met at a London hotel in the early 1970s, and in his usual perceptive manner Clough immediately touched on Moore's one unfulfilled ambition: a League Championship medal. 'Come to Derby and I'll win you one,' promised the game's most controversial manager. And Moore wanted to go.

A month after winning the World Cup, Hurst, Moore and Peters were back in training for West Ham. (Sport & General)

Moore receives a gold medal from Dr Borg Olivier, Malta's Minister of Education and Tourism, to mark his selection as Player of Players in the World Cup.

But the move was again blocked by Greenwood, to Moore's eternal disappointment, and he was to move on at the end of that season to finish his career at Fulham, a cherished title medal ambition left by the wayside.

Yet back in the World Cup aftermath, all Moore had to look forward to was the 1968 European Championships for which qualification was via the Home International Championship. To Moore's irritation, England lost to Scotland at Wembley in 1967, with Denis Law scoring one of the goals in a 3–2 victory which the fanatical Scots believed made them the World Champions. What it didn't do was prevent England from qualifying for Europe. After a home and away quarter-final success

The World Champions show off their prize. Back row, from the left: Harold Shepherdson (trainer), Nobby Stiles, Roger Hunt, Gordon Banks, Jack Charlton, George Cohen, Ray Wilson and Alf Ramsey (manager); front row: Martin Peters, Geoff Hurst, Bobby Moore, Alan Ball and Bobby Charlton. *(Hulton Deutsch)*

(Far left) Pals on and off the pitch. Moore and Jimmy Greaves clash during a London derby at White Hart Lane in 1969.

The captain looks on as his England teammates enjoy a game of cards en route to Romania in 1968. From the left: Brian Labone, Martin Peters, Geoff Hurst, Bobby Charlton and (back to camera) Alan Mullery.

against Spain, Moore took his side to meet Yugoslavia in the semi-final in Florence.

The Yugoslavs were a dangerous mix, not short on physical aggression, yet blessed with abundant skill. They adopted spoiling tactics to try to deny England winning the game with a goal for which Moore accepted responsibility. He failed to reach high enough for a long ball from midfield. Dragon Djazic was in behind him, the goal was scored and

England were out, a defeat also soured by the sending off of Alan Mullery.

But there was the defence of the World Cup to look forward to, and that had always been Ramsey's priority concern. He now had a knighthood for his 1966 achievement and Moore had been awarded an OBE. Ramsey had made fine adjustments to the England squad as injury and the march of time accounted for players like Cohen, Wilson, Stiles and Hunt. Greaves annoyed Ramsey by saying he didn't want to be selected unless he was in the team. A new side emerged which included Keith Newton. Brian Labone, Mullery, Francis Lee and Colin Bell. Yet, during the 19-match period between the European Championships of 1968 and the World Cup of 1970, while the experimentation continued, England lost only once, to Brazil in Rio de Janeiro.

England found themselves drawn with Brazil, Romania and Czechoslovakia in a group

With Eusebio of Portugal who collected an overseas award during the 1966 BBC presentations. *(George Herringshaw)*

(Far left) And the trophies roll in ... Moore collects the BBC Sports Personality of the Year award. *(George Herringshaw)*

We can win it again ... Moore and Sir Alf agree that they can retain the World Cup in Mexico as Moore collects a Sportsman of the Month award from his international manager at London's Sportsman Club in 1970.

that was considered testing, though they were expected to qualify for the next round. The preparation for playing at altitude had been meticulous, not least in choosing warm-up games at height in Colombia and Ecuador. But that decision was to backfire – on Moore in particular.

After two weeks' training in Mexico, the side headed for Bogotá to test the effectiveness of their preparations in a match situation. But at a small jeweller's shop in the Tequendama Hotel, on the very day England checked in, Moore and Bobby Charlton looked at a possible present for the later's wife, Norma. It was 18 May 1970, a date that was to be etched in Moore's memory.

For, no sooner had England's two foremost players left the shop to sit in the foyer just yards away, than accusations were levelled by the shop assistant, Clara Padilla, that an emerald and diamond bracelet had been stolen. Police were called in, Sir Alf intervened and statements were taken. The game went ahead with Moore playing, England winning 4–0, and the squad set off for Equador to record another victory, this time by two goals.

Yet en route back to Mexico, the plane had to stop over again in Bogatá. But so

Moore relaxes by watching a rodeo in Mexico City.

(Above right) Moore feels the heat during a break in training for the match with Czechoslovakia.

(Right) Moore in action for England in 1970. (*Colorsport*)

convinced was Ramsey that the matter of the bracelet was now closed that he took the team back to the same hotel to relax by watching a western film.

But while the team viewed the movie, Moore was whisked away to a police station, supposedly to confirm his earlier statement. That afternoon, the plane left for Mexico without its captain, detained and still listening to the debate between lawyers and police at 10 pm that night. Eventually, he was taken and kept under house arrest as the charade

unfolded over the next four days of endless questions, noisy and animated conversations, uncoordinated investigations and even a reconstruction of the alleged crime in the very shop where the supposed theft had taken place, with Moore cross-examing the shop assistant. Moore took the entire ordeal in his stride, strolling with his guards and showing the kind of unflappable front that enabled him to cope with all situations on the football pitch.

Eventually he was released unconditionally and the Colombian soccer fans, sensing Moore had been framed, turned up in droves to send him on his way to re-join his teammates in Guadalajara.

The attempt to disturb the concentration of perhaps the world's most gifted defender had failed, for when the Champions set out to defend their trophy against Romania, Moore was there along with six other members of the 1966 winning side.

'We felt we were as well prepared, if not better, than any other nation. We all felt in great shape despite the altitude and the heat. I looked at the squad and felt we were stronger than in 1966. In fact, we felt it was the best squad in

England's history,' Moore said. Yet it was not an auspicious beginning, a 1–0 win with Hurst scoring the goal against a side playing defensively.

It was the match that followed that was billed as the meeting of the Champions against the potential Champions and it fulfilled all the expectations. It lives in the memory for so many reasons, but the two principal ones were Banks' remarkable save to deny Pelé, and the great Brazilian's exchange of shirts with Moore at the end of the game, the expressions of mutual admiration saying so much. 'The finest defender I played against,' said Pelé. The sentiment, in terms of Pelé's outrageous talent, was reciprocated by Moore. Few doubted then that the two teams would meet again, probably in the final. England won their remaining game against Czechoslovakia with a Clarke penalty and the stage was set for a quarter-final against the Germans.

This time, on the very day of the match, an attack of gastroenteritis put Banks out of the side and Peter Bonetti deputised at the last possible moment. But he had done it several times before over the previous four years and there was no cause to doubt he could do it again. Moore was in control of the game and goals from Mullery and Peters had England in comfortable superiority with 20 minutes remaining.

Sir Stanley Rous, one of the great figures of English and world soccer meets another, Bobby Moore. (Sport & General)

But then Sir Alf, who also believed the game won, made his fatal error and prepared to take off Bobby Charlton and Peters to conserve their energy for the semi-final, and bring on Bell and Hunter. 'I could understand his thinking at the time,' Moore was to reflect. 'But really Bobby was one of the fittest men in the squad and as he crossed the touchline Franz Beckenbauer looked like a ton had been lifted from his shoulders. He started to come at us for the first time.' And, in the 70th minute, the Germans brought on Grobowski and he began tormenting the tiring England side. Beckenbauer pulled a goal back from a shot that Bonetti ought to have saved. But it suddenly put England on a poor psychological footing, as the substitutions were made. Uwe Seeler headed a late equaliser straining to reach the ball that looped over Bonetti, his concentration adrift.

The extra time was never going to compare with Wembley four years earlier. England were mentally beaten and another goal prodded in by Gerd Muller knocked out the Champions. Moore was numb; Bonetti was silent; Ball was in tears. There was nothing to say. England had simply thrown it away.

As Moore recovered from his disappointment on the beach at Acapulco, having stayed on to see Brazil defeat Italy in the final, his mind wandered to the future, and there was no reason for him not to feel his international career would not continue. But what of Sir Alf, the man who made him skipper and who showed a loyalty that sometimes extended beyond the parameters of common sense?

Back in England, Moore was to run into problems in January 1971 for a late-night drinking session in Blackpool prior to a third round FA Cup match. It seemed improbable that the man so dedicated to his profession should be out breaking curfew, even for a few beers that were just the norm for him. It was an incident that assumed a greater import

Sir Alf with his England squad in 1971.

than it really merited and Moore was stung by a two-week suspension which left a question mark over his fitness for a forthcoming European Championship match against Malia. Moore missed the game with Mullery, later to be his Fulham teammate, taking over the captaincy.

England's qualifying competition for those Championships turned into another nightmare for Ramsey. England drew West Germany again in the quarter-finals and in the home leg Ramsey made a calamitous error, partnering Moore with Norman Hunter when Roy McFarland was ruled unfit. To make matters worse, he chose not to select a ball-winner, and Gunther Netzer came to Wembley thinking it was Christmas. He ran riot at Wembley in a game Moore looked back on as one of his worst in the England shirt, though he knew that he and his defenders were getting virtually no help from midfield.

Germany won 3–1, with Moore admitting to one mistake and Emlyn Hughes

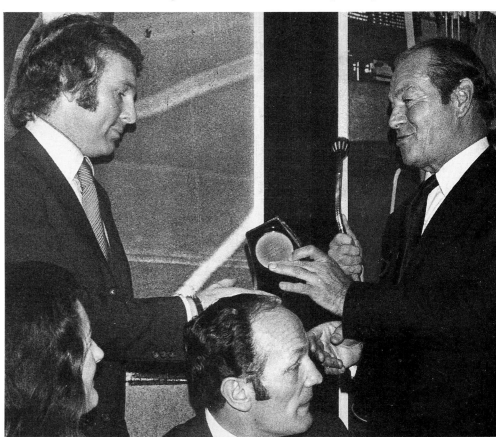

shouldering the blame for another, with the third being a penalty. In the return leg Ramsey sought a negative result, sensing that victory was beyond his team. For Moore and for his manager, the memories of European Championships were to be no happier than those of Bobby Robson in 1988 and Graham Taylor in 1992.

Moore receives his 'Top Ten' award from Beaverbrook Newspapers proprietor Sir Max Aitken for reaching the World Cup quarter-final in 1970.

It was downhill from there for Ramsey, and to some extent for Moore also. The new World Cup challenge for 1974 embraced Wales and Poland and there was no reason at the outset for England to be too concerned. They defeated Wales 1–0 at Cardiff, but were stunned by a John Toshack goal in the return, with Hunter grateful to get an equaliser. England thought that they were off the hook, especially when Wales then held Poland to a draw. But it was in Chorzow, the grim industrial Polish city, that the England manager got it all wrong again by playing for safety. Mike Channon was left out for the more

defensive Peter Storey and the defence was instructed to keep it tight and not to concede. But concede they did in the first half from a free kick to the near post that brushed Moore as it found the target. But worse was to follow for England's skipper in the second half. He was caught in possession by Polish flyer Lubanski and the game was lost. It was to be the beginning of the end for both Moore and Ramsey.

He played again against Russia four days after the Polish debacle and again in Turin a further four days later, when he broke Bobby Charlton's record of 106 caps. It was not a happy match for him, however, one of the goals flying in through his legs and there were mutterings of discontent, even from Ramsey, for the first time in 10 years about his skipper. It was the last night of his final England tour and he drank through the night with Ball for company. A great deal of soul-searching followed. He was still named in the squad for the first match of the following

season, at home to Austria, but when Alf came and sat next to him on the bus after training he sensed the worst. 'I've got a disappointment for you,' he said. Moore barely heard the explanations about how well Hunter had been playing for Leeds.

(Left) Moore's England career was drawing to a close by the time of this Home International against Scotland in May 1973, but the timing was still there and pacey winger Willie Morgan could find no way through. (*Sport & General*)

(Below left) Clowning with Rodney Marsh during England training. They were soon to be club colleagues as well.

(Right) Moore and a long-haired Alan Ball in Moscow before their 1973 international with Russia.

Moore asked point-blank if that was the end, but Ramsey insisted that if England qualified for the finals he would be skipper in West Germany. Before that, Poland had to be beaten at Wembley and Moore could only watch it from the bench. Hunter, by the worst of ironies, gave away a goal to the Poles with a mistake similar to the one Moore had made in Poland. England were out, defied by a goalkeeper called Tomaszewski. There was not to be a fourth World Cup for Bobby Moore. Indeed, there was to be just one more international, fittingly at home to Italy. England lost 1–0 and Moore knew that was the end, though nobody actually told him. It was the end, too, for Alf after the very next match in Portugal. He selected a brand new side but it didn't save his neck. The Football Association dropped the axe. An era had ended.

It ended at West Ham, too, as Moore made one last change to his footballing career,

Moore's 107th cap – a total which took him past the previous record-holder, Bobby Charlton – was against Italy. (*Colorsport*)

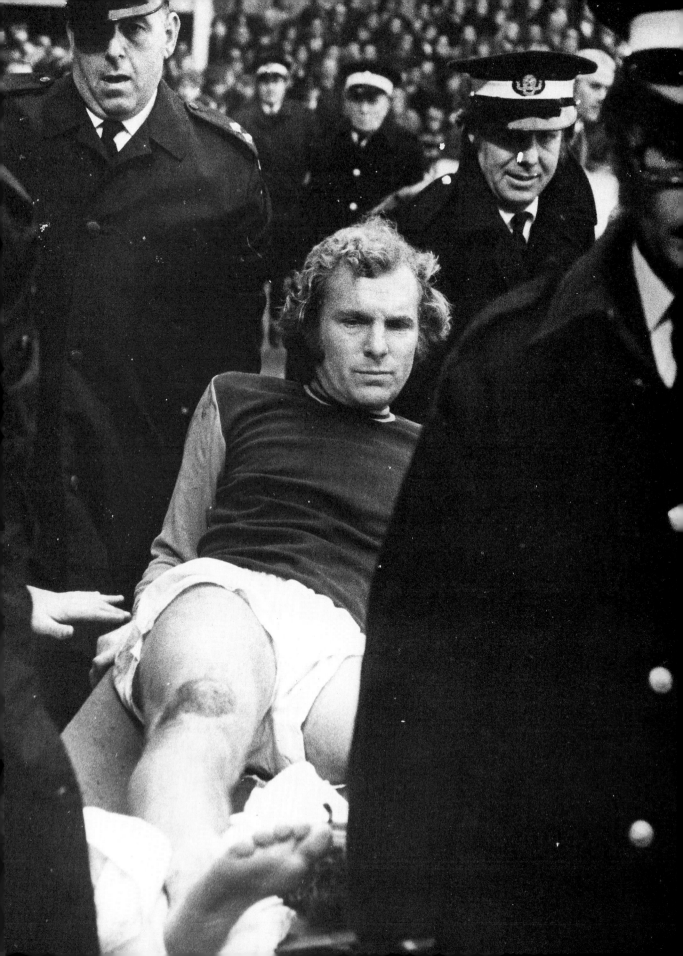

joining Fulham for £25,000 when he would have preferred to be reunited with his old mentor Malcolm Allison at Crystal Palace. Fulham manager Alec Stock sent Mullery along with the club secretary to complete the signing, determined to make sure there was no change of heart on Moore's part. A career at West Ham spanning 16 years and 642 first team matches was over.

He quickly felt at home at Craven Cottage despite a catastrophic debut in which the side lost 4–0 at home.

Having recently joined Fulham, Moore learns some close teamwork with the club's new Danish international signing Flemming Hanssen and captain Alan Mullery. (*Sport & General*)

But at the start of the next season he and Mullery would put together an FA Cup run which staggered even them. They needed replay after replay to account for Hull City and Nottingham Forest, now managed by Clough. They went to Everton and won with two goals from Viv Busby and Moore was delighted by the spirit within the club. Then it was another away-day at Carlisle, the prelude to a semi-final against Birmingham City at neutral Hillsborough. Another draw there sent them to a victorious replay at Maine Road. And, by the most remarkable of ironies, the team they would meet at Wembley was West Ham.

Rodney Marsh, back from Tampa Bay Rowdies, signs for Fulham in 1976 to team up with England colleague Moore.

(Left) Moore becomes a Fulham player.

At the end of his career, Moore posed for the cameras with a replica of the trophy that had meant so much to him. *(Sport & General)*

Moore and Mullery did their best to keep the rest of the team relaxed before the match, but it was almost impossible. 'Nice to be home again,' said Moore as the coach arrived at the stadium. The message from manager Alec Stock was a short one: 'See this old suit. I've had it 16 years. Go out and do it so the old fellow can buy a new one.'

That was the way it was at Fulham. Take your football seriously, but do keep a smile on your face. In many ways it was a fitting atmosphere for Moore to wind down from a career that had touched the very highest peaks. And this Wembley match was just a little bonus, a nostalgic trip to the pitch where he achieved his highest honour. Maybe he didn't move around it with quite the same swagger and authority, but this was nine years on.

Stock's last words to his team were 'Remember to enjoy it lads.'

The familiar noise filtered down the Wembley tunnel, a sound that had filled Moore's head so many times and which set his own adrenalin pumping. He and Mullery, the two old heads, were in control in a goalless first half when Fulham felt they had the upper hand. But then at the start of the second half, disaster struck Moore's boys. Peter Mellor could only block a shot from Billy Jennings and Alan Taylor prodded it home. And then, just five minutes later, Mellor failed to hang on to a shot from Graham Paddon and Taylor was on hand again. There was no coming back for Fulham and, for once, Moore climbed the steps as a loser. It was a new experience late in his career and not one he cared for. He

declined the drinks, the aftermath and the consoling slaps on the back.

Moore's swansong was for the Portland Timbers in the American Soccer League. (Colorsport)

Bobby Moore was a poor loser, but it was not an experience he suffered often. He knew the time to call it a day was at hand, and he left the game he had enriched quietly and with dignity. Right till the end with Fulham, he would drive from Essex daily and be at the training ground before those who lived just around the corner. 'He's a true professional, you see,' Stock once told me. 'There are some things you don't lose in life.' The losing battle for Bobby Moore came much later, but the memory will live wherever and whenever there is football discussed.

PART THREE

BOBBY MOORE

THE MAN

BY JAMES LAWTON

CHAPTER SEVEN

MOURNING THE END OF A DREAM

W hen Bobby Moore was gone, finally; when the bleak rituals at a small, private funeral in Putney were done on the late winter morning, there was a sad, slightly numb, national consensus that there had rarely been such grieving.

There had been no scream of anguish, no Valentino graveyard scenes, but feelings had gone to the bone sure enough. There had been a huge collective sigh, an overpowering sense that something had changed, something in ourselves, perhaps even that some of our dreams had been shattered.

Of course there has been other terrible, random grief. Bobby Moore was not the first to suffer an untimely death –

Stephanie leaves Putney Vale Crematorium after the funeral

sooner or later, each of us is obliged to tread the same path. So, in every corner of the land, every day, there are competing sadnesses, inevitable pockets of the rage and disbelief which come with sudden death.

But these are the careless arrows of fate, to be suffered in the timeless way by small groups of the bereaved, isolated in their pain. The mourning of Bobby Moore, we knew straightaway, was something different.

It was more personal than the passing of a great warrior statesman like Churchill or an artist like Nureyev, men we might admire, even love for different reasons, but whom we never felt we could touch, or say, 'How's it going, mate?' and know that we would receive a reply. But it was less intense, much less engulfing, albeit more complicated, than the desolation of suddenly losing a close and beloved relative.

For so many, Bobby Moore's death in his prime was a bell tolling for their youth, their happiest, most comfortable days, which would stretch, it once seemed, forever. They felt this with such poignant force that younger generations could only stop and ask, 'Who was this man, this football player?'

Moore's popularity transcended club barriers as this tribute from Tottenham fans shows

Clearly, he had an extraordinary quality. His death touched people so deeply: Bosnia, the economy, even the trauma of little Jamie Bulger's murder, were swept out of the news bulletins and the headlines. The prime minister, mending fences with a new president in Washington, broke off to make a personal statement. What was it about Bobby Moore that carried him over the decades, so serene in the affection and deep respect of his countrymen and women?

Bobby Moore was still picking up awards for his sporting achievements as late as 1990.
(Sport & General)

A small child wears her
Hammers colours amid
the mass of flowers...

The first answer was erroneous. In a rush of emotion, some said he was as much a saint as a warrior. We got that wrong.

Bobby Moore was not a saint. He was as vulnerable as the next man. He had his

...and an older fan remembers.

scrapes and his disasters, the pain of looking at himself and wondering what he had done with his life. But somehow he convinced us he would always come shining through, as he did that summer's day at Wembley in 1966 when he lifted up the World Cup and felt the embrace of his nation. Only now, when life has given its cruellest cut, has that embrace been forcibly loosened.

Bobby Moore linked us to one of the happiest days in our national life. He didn't win a war or change history. He won a football game, but it was a great game, a great day, and it made everyone feel good. We didn't want to lose that feeling. As long as Bobby was around, straight-backed, cheery in his understated way, riding the blows, re-arranging his

life, the feeling we had that distant day would remain – my own wife, no football fan, knitting for our first, unborn child wept with joy when he wiped his hands clean before meeting the Queen. He was a symbol of better, more optimistic days.

Looking at 'Mooro', sipping his lager, nodding an acknowledgement with his puckish grin and unbreachable dignity, who really cared if he never walked the halls of football authority? Leave that to the little men with the fancy titles and the clipper boards and the jargon.

Who cared if his business career seemed to be one extended Bermuda triangle? Who cared if, when times were not so good, he was sports editor of a tabloid which ran pictures of the fattest woman in the world and told of sex romps in a baronial house, when all the posh papers could provide were meaningless columns by current players who would never know what Moore did, what Moore meant?

Bobby Moore, as his hero Frank Sinatra sang, could take the blows. He went about his life with control, with a sense that the world could hurt him, disappoint him, leave him quietly despairing in the small hours of the night, but it couldn't break him.

Maybe it was this that prompted Ray Wilson, the great full back who shared Moore's day of triumph at Wembley, to indulge, long after the first joy of victory was spent, in a moment of black humour.

Wilson, whose football after-life has been spent as an undertaker, handed Moore his business card and said, 'You don't look good, better put my card in your top pocket.' Wilson's joke was that Moore always looked good, but for the brief, worrying time two years ago when he had his first surgery for stomach cancer, and in the final, mercifully quick, decline when the disease spread to his liver. He always looked like a million dollars.

Wilson's joke detonates bizarrely now. The devastation which gripped the land – and was expressed so graphically on the bloodless, dull-eyed faces of men like Bobby Charlton, Nobby Stiles, Geoff Hurst and Martin Peters – flowed from Ray Wilson's breezy assumption that no man was less susceptible to the possibilities of his own mortality than his former captain.

As a mark of respect, West Ham abandoned the No. 6 shirt - worn with such distinction by Moore - and Ian Bishop wore the No. 12 shirt instead.

Moore would go on and on. We would go about our business, winning and losing, and he would be there – a comfortable piece of furniture in our lives, someone we could trust.

His wife Stephanie's farewell card was touching and beautiful and ultimately personal: 'Always be close,' she wrote. 'You are my everything …' Bobby Moore could never mean as much to us, and sometimes he was on the edge of our consciousness. It was when he was gone, or perhaps when we knew for sure that he was going, that the meaning of our

Arsenal and Leeds players give Bobby Moore a minute's silence. The spectators were utterly quiet at Highbury and all around the country where similar respects were paid

particular loss came so sharply into focus.

Beyond his flesh and blood, no one was so broken by his death as the two men who in some ways were the most unlikely elder statesmen of his life.

Malcolm Allison sobbed uncontrollably, while Noel Cantwell was plunged back into the deep grief he had been dealing with, sometimes well, sometimes not so well, since the death of his son in a car crash five years ago.

'Young Bobby' had been the kid trailing at their elbows back at West Ham United, when he came scrubbed clean and gleaming with hope and ambition and an inquisitiveness which sometimes plagued them but was never rebuffed because this worldly pair saw in it something that was as hard and as bright as a diamond.

He followed them everywhere, on bus-rides home with Allison, hitching rides with Cantwell. Once he went to Cantwell's tailor and ordered a jacket identical to one recently purchased by the big Irishman. He wore it, blue eyes shining with pleasure, shameless in his sartorial mimicry of one of his heroes.

He was the most eager pupil Allison and Cantwell had ever seen. And they were

The minute's silence is observed by old friends and colleagues. From the left: Hurst, Frank Lampard, Greenwood, Peters, Harry Redknapp, Billy Bonds, Ronnie Boyce.

masters of the universe, men who would explain the mysteries of their magical kingdom. There were so many mysteries to unravel, methodically, relentlessly.

A few days before he died, Moore went with Allison to the Fleet Street office of Barry Gold, the solicitor who is organising Allison's testimonial year. 'I was shocked by Bobby's appearance,' said Allison. 'He had been away in Florida and the change in him since I stayed with him at New Year was devastating. At the New Year, he still looked good, he was pushing back our worst fears. At breakfast, he produced rows of vitamin pills, other pills, and took them quite systematically. He laughed about it. Then he went for a run. But that morning in Fleet Street I knew he was going and I could hardly take it in.

'When we finished our business, I said, "Come on, Bobby, let's get some lunch." I didn't want to let him leave me, I wanted to get hold of him, wrap my arms around him. But he said, in his matter-of-fact way, that he had to go and do a broadcast. He had to fly. But Bobby wasn't flying anymore, and he walked off into the street and when he was gone it occurred to me that I might never see him again.

'It all came back to me, his life, the way he had always been, and it was just too terrible to think that we wouldn't have him anymore …'

Moore had followed Allison and Cantwell more slavishly than any lap-dog and so, of course, they watched in wonder when he grew so strong, so firmly directed, so insistent that he would achieve all his goals.

He even joined them on his honeymoon, expressly against the orders of his first wife Tina's mother.

Both men chuckle at the memory. Cantwell says: 'Bobby's mother-in-law had heard we would be in Majorca with our wives when Bobby, who was then just 20, and Tina came out for their honeymoon and she contacted us both and said, "Just don't get in touch with them."

'We didn't. Maggie and I, and Malcolm and his first wife Beth were staying in a place called Puerto Soller, quite a modest place. Bobby and Tina were up the island, living a little more swankily. So we were surprised when Bobby and Tina showed up on our little beach. Of course one thing led to another, and I suppose we three finished up drinking a few glasses of champagne. Tina got very angry, as did Maggie and Beth.

'The upshot was that Bobby finished up sleeping with Mal and me, while Tina slept with Maggie and Beth. There were quite a few hot words but on the following day peace reigned. It was a curious thing, but our lives had become interwoven for some time.'

Allison had the first contact. West Ham's manager Ted Fenton asked him to supervise the training of local schoolboys twice a week. Some great talent had been trawled from the fertile streets of East London and the Essex sprawl. Outstanding among them was a boy called Georgie Fenn. He had played for England Schoolboys, scored goals with great freedom and was also a natural sprinter, a fine cricketer and a boxer of some promise. 'George was Roy of the Rovers. Bobby, in terms of natural talent, was simply another hopeful kid who was not so quick on his feet,' recalls Allison.

'After a while Ted Fenton called me up to his office and asked about the kids. I mentioned a few names, including Bobby's, and then Fenton said, "But what about Georgie Fenn, everyone wants to sign Georgie." I told him that I didn't think Fenn would make it, there was something wrong with his attitude. But I said that Bobby Moore could make a great player. Fenton shook his head.

'You could understand Fenton's disappointment. Georgie Fenn could have been a George Best, but he didn't have the appetite. It was as simple as that, you could see it like reading an open book. Bobby was precisely the opposite.'

Given this background, the famous occasion when Cantwell had to recommend either Moore or Allison for a place against Manchester United was a terrible dilemma. Allison ached to play, to taste the big time after the long months of despair in a sanatorium in Surrey. But Cantwell suggested Moore – and he was on his way.

The Boys of '66 reunited. Back row: Wilson, Jack Charlton, Hurst, Peters; middle: Stiles, Cohen, Hunt, Banks, Maurice Lindley; front: Bobby Charlton, Moore, Sir Alf, Harold Sheperdson, Ball.

The bonds between these men, shaped under such circumstances, withstood the years. Moore had criticisms of Allison's extravagant lifestyle, questioning his ability as a coach to live – and drink – with the players and still retain his authority and power to instil discipline. But whenever they saw each other, the mutual affection welled.

Cantwell, like Allison, groped to absorb the news of Moore's death: 'He was so much part of our lives. He never missed a birthday of our children and when we lost our son in the car crash, he simply came to our house and asked what he could do. He was family and he was something else, something solid but glamorous, and whatever happened to him, you knew that in a way he would always be blessed, always be special.'

The pain Allison felt when he saw Bobby Moore walk away from him, forever, on that Fleet Street morning, kindled a thousand memories, and most of them were a celebration of a fine spirit and a great friendship.

'Not so long ago,' he remembers, 'I had some success with the Portuguese team Vitoria Setubal. I managed to take them back up to the Portuguese First Division. Everyone was thrilled. We clinched promotion playing on the island of Madeira. When we got back to Lisbon airport, there was a great cheering mob.

'In the middle of the crowd, I saw Lynn [his companion and the mother of his young daughter Gina] standing with Bobby and Stephanie. Bobby had a big grin on his face and a couple of bottles of champagne in his hands. He said, "I suppose we'd better go somewhere and drink this stuff." I said, "That's wonderful, Bobby."

'Wonderful, Bobby . . .' It was a phrase that came easily to the lips of all who knew him. He was not a saint, perhaps not always the hero we painted him to be in the first rush of grief, but he was wrapped in a quality that was a kind of wonder. He came into so many lives, and when you look at men like Allison and Cantwell, rugged old survivors of the game of football and life, you know he will never be replaced.

CHAPTER EIGHT

WALKING THE NARROW LINE

Bobby Moore was a knight in shining armour, a true arrow, a man who walked effortlessly through the perils of sporting celebrity. He was someone who, when George Best was squandering a talent that briefly illuminated the world of football, faultlessly negotiated the minefield. Bobby Moore always did the right thing.

Bobby Moore was the warrior captain of England, and also the very nice, uncomplicated boy next door. That was the image, and it was one that Moore strived to achieve, for reasons we will never know, but they were buried deeply in his origins in a little street in Barking. But, as is so often the case in these matters, there was a gap between the image and the reality.

Bobby Moore ventured into that area where the image no longer holds true, where sometimes demons came out to dance so vigorously on his exemplary parade that those who loved him most, not for the glory that reflected from him but because of what he was, feared that he might go under. But he came through those trials.

There was a danger that he might pile up too much stress in the need to be the good man, the good pro, the model player, the model husband, the model national hero. He might be too busy being the model *something* that the substance of him would be worn away. It didn't happen, and this – his closest friends will always say – was his greatest achievement. In the end, after the pain and fear of lost horizons, the collapse of his relationship with his first wife Tina, which as a 20-year-old he imagined would last for ever, and several business disasters, Bobby Moore finally located reality, the real place that lay between what he wanted and that which he thought the world wanted him to be.

Through it all there was an enduring theme. Painstakingly fastidious in his dress, his habits, he was obsessed by appearance and the need to look right. Of this aspect of his life, in all the tributes and memories that poured out when Bobby Moore died, nothing was more telling than an anecdote offered by Michael Hart, football correspondent of the London *Evening Standard* and, like Moore, a graduate of the hard, warm life of East London.

Playing with George Best in the Sports Aid Charity match at Wembley in May 1986.

As a young sports news agency reporter assigned to Moore's club West Ham, Hart made the arduous, daily trek by train and bus to the training ground in Chadwell Heath. One day, the young reporter, who was paid just a few pounds a week for long hours – he had been told, like most eagerly aspiring reporters that he was lucky to have the privilege of being taught his inky trade – was telling Moore, the relatively wealthy young football star, about the complications of his travelling arrangements. Moore, typically, offered to give him a lift whenever he could.

On one journey, Moore tentatively mentioned that perhaps

Read all about it ... Moore launches his autobiography by Jeff Powell with George Best (left) and Gerry Francis.

Hart should smarten himself up a little, perhaps buy a suit and give himself a little more gravitas in the wardrobe. Hart explained the economic realities as seen by a young reporter. A few days later, Hart was stunned when Moore pointed to a suit and several shirts and ties neatly folded on the back seat and said, 'They're for you.'

Appearances were by no means everything to Bobby Moore, but they were desperately important. They were a badge, a covering note about what lay inside; perhaps he felt a little of the impulse that drove careworn Lancashire housewives to shine the worn steps at their front doors.

Long after the victories had been won, the defeats absorbed and the compromises made with reality, Moore still needed his privacy, an opportunity to be truly himself – a place where he could not be touched. After the doctors had told him his fate, he said to his close friend Jeff Powell of the *Daily Mail*, 'It's cancer – it's nothing to be ashamed of is it?'

Another intimate friend, Terry Venables, read that quote with

Bobby is part of the Swinging Sixties with this model line-up.

a shock of possible recognition of the reason for something that had intrigued, and at times dismayed, him all along. 'I'd always wondered about a certain stiffness in Bobby at certain times, a high guard. He was such a lovely man but sometimes, if you introduced someone new to his company, he would be stiff and edgy. Then he would have one lager, maybe two and his face would relax, his eyes would start to shine. He needed that

lubrication; he never had a problem with drink, but maybe he could have done, if he hadn't been so strong, if he hadn't had a sure knowledge of who he was and what he always wanted to be. The lagers didn't change Bobby, but they relaxed him, they made things seem a little easier.'

Venables, an unusually perceptive young player for Tottenham, had attempted to change the course of Moore's club career at an early point. He had told Moore of his club's high regard for the emerging West Ham star. It certainly triggered Moore's interest and had it borne fruit in the transfer market, the persistent thread of professional frustration which ran through Bobby's club career would have been neatly picked out.

But West Ham manager Ron Greenwood, whose football knowledge Moore greatly respected, saw the player as a cornerstone of his hopes of assembling a consistent team – something to build from the early flying success in the FA Cup and the European Cup-Winners' Cup. Greenwood shooed away Tottenham, as he would much later shoo away Brian Clough, who wanted Moore as the elder statesman, the on-field educator of his new champions Derby County. The rejection of Spurs closed in for Moore for a decade, leaving him to ponder what might have been. This may, in a fleeting way, have been expressed in the kind of commonplace incident which occurs regularly at most clubs, but which, when it involved Moore, seemed to have much greater implications.

It was an essentially innocent business, but it threw pressure on

Bobby coaching schoolboys at Forest School, Snaresbrook

Bobby launches the Bobby Moore Coaching Scheme. Back row: Phil Beal, Paddy Crerand, Malcolm Macdonald, Martin Chivers, Ron Yeats, Terry Paine, Mike Summerbee. Front: Ron Springett, Moore, Joe Mercer, Frank McLintock, Ian St John.

both his marriage to Tina and his standing as one of the game's great professionals. It happened on a Friday night in Blackpool in January 1971. Moore broke club rules. Instead of observing club curfew on the eve of a third round FA Cup tie – West Ham, as was usually the case, desperately needed Cup success to redeem another mediocre league season – he went to the nightclub of boxer Brian London. West Ham were thrashed and news of Moore's Friday night/Saturday morning sojourn leaked out. Fleet Street lapped up the story. An angry West Ham fan threw a stone through the window of Moore's sports shop opposite Upton Park. Moore always wanted everything to look right. This didn't.

Moore had gone to the nightclub with Jimmy Greaves and Brian Dear, teammates whose liking for a drink was legendary within the game, and, critically, the young player from Bermuda, Clyde Best. He told Jeff Powell, his 1976 biographer, 'I suppose we all realised at the time we were leaving ourselves vulnerable. People will throw up their hands in horror at the thought of professional sportsmen going for a drink the night before a game. But it was hardly a diabolical liberty. In fact, we thought very little about it. We were in bed by 1.30 and got up about 10 the next morning. That's a good night's sleep by anyone's standards.

'We're talking about two glasses of wine and a few lagers. Not one of us felt we had jeopardised the team's chances. No player would do that on purpose. If a player did, I would consider him warped. I wouldn't want him in my team, he shouldn't be part of my team. The problem was not the drinking but the result.'

The result was 4–0 for Blackpool. It was not even the Blackpool of Matthews and Mortensen and the bewitching Ernie Taylor, but scuffling heirs to that great tradition. It was a disaster for West Ham United, the team who in Moore, Geoff Hurst and Martin Peters had provided a spine running through England's World Cup triumph.

'There was only one winner from the start,' Moore recalled. 'Ron Greenwood was upset with the performance because it was hardly a performance at all. It was a sick trip home but nothing much was said and that seemed to be the end of it.' Moore didn't know that the trap was already baited. In the anger of defeat, the word flowed through West Ham's travelling support that the 'lads' had been boozing late in a Blackpool nightclub. One of the fans carried his outrage all the way to Greenwood's office at Upton Park. It is a fixture of the football manager's life, the 'ratting' call, often punctuated by the dropping of coins in a public phone box. This player was thrown out of that nightclub, that player had a fight in this local pub, another was down at the bookie's.

More often than not, the manager sweeps up this minutiae of common man's failings, says he will look into it, and goes about his business as though the call had never been placed. Moore said, 'Normally, Ron would have dismissed that sort of thing. From that aspect, Ron was too big a man to have truck with people phoning in or calling to tell tales on players just because the team had a bad result. This time, though, the club chairman Reg Pratt walked into the manager's office in the middle of the heated discussion and the midst of his own disappointment with the Cup defeat. He demanded to know what the fuss was about.'

There were phone calls coming in to the players from Fleet Street newspapers. The story was running, the headlines would be huge. Moore's image took a hammering. He was suspended for two weeks, fined a week's wages, wages which seem quite pathetic now – £200. Less than five years earlier he had become a *bona fide* national hero and household name.

Moore proving his fitness in 1973 in the TV show 'Superstars'.

Of course it was the merest squall in a career which spoke of a

commitment, an understanding of priorities, which was in many ways phenomenal. But it took us to the heart, the central dilemma of Bobby Moore's life. It revealed much about the way he walked the line, a line which his great friend Jimmy Greaves at one stage crossed to the point where he might have destroyed everything he valued in life. It was also this line across which Moore's brilliant West Ham teammate Johnny 'Budgie' Byrne was lured to professional destruction.

Moore, we can assume, had trouble getting the balance right at times of stress. But he managed it, with skill and much character. He always saw that there was a limit, while players like George Best didn't.

Reflecting on the Blackpool affair, he also said, 'Of course some players have damaged

Moore and Greaves sign autographs in 1972 after the launch of Greaves' East Ham Travel Agency.

themselves by too much social life. Two of the best players I know, Jim Baxter and Budgie Byrne, did themselves no favours. But everyone is different. A drink helps me to unwind in the way it obviously helped Dave Mackay. You were always hearing stories of Dave being picked up off the pavement up and down Tottenham High Road every night of the week. It didn't stop him being a great player for Spurs every time he went out on the pitch.

'As long as you don't regularly drink to excess, the problem is mental rather than physical. When I was a young player starting out, I wouldn't dream of taking a drink after Thursday night. I wasn't really used to it because my dad never drank at all. Yet you saw the senior pros going for a couple of beers on a Friday night and slowly it dawned on you that it was all an attitude of mind. At first you don't do things in case they affect you. Then you realise everyone's different and it's an individual decision.'

There were, inevitably, other scrapes, notably an earlier one with England manager Alf Ramsey back in 1964, when Moore was still on the foothills of his climb to the peaks of football celebrity he would share with such as Pelé and Franz Beckenbauer.

Imagine the competing pressures on Moore as he joined the England squad fresh from West Ham's Cup final triumph over Preston North End. He had just finished another hard, triumphant season, but he had to knuckle down again. Moore checked into White's Hotel, a rambling place on the Bayswater Road, four days before the team were due to play against Portugal in Lisbon. Portugal meant more in international terms then. Their leading team, Benfica, were a major force in Europe; they had great men like Eusebio, Coluna and Simoes. But Moore, as any young man might be, was in celebration mode.

When he took a stroll down the Bayswater Road on the bright spring night, his companions included an emerging list of all-time greats of English football: Bobby Charlton, Gordon Banks, George Eastham, Jimmy Greaves, Ray Wilson and the brilliant but erratic club teammate Byrne. After a dinner under the stern gaze of team manager Alf Ramsey, they were merely stretching their legs before observing an 11.30 curfew. But the

With Pelé during the 1986 World Cup in Mexico.

air was warm, Hyde Park smelled sharp and sweet in the spring, and there were no dissenters when it was suggested – possibly by Byrne – that a little drink be taken in the West End.

It was, rather like the one in Blackpool, a modest assault on the nightspots. They returned to the hotel shortly after midnight, a little more than half an hour past curfew. But Ramsey was more attentive to such detail than Greenwood, less inclined to assume the best of men he admired. He ordered a midnight check and the empty beds were noted. When they returned to their rooms, they found their passports neatly placed on the pillows. The line had been drawn, with shuddering force, for young Bobby Moore. He played in the game, played well, but he never forgot how close he had come to wrecking it all.

If Ramsey had done more than throw a scare, if he had been annoyed enough to turn against a young man who had won his immediate trust, the glittering prizes awaiting Bobby Moore might have been snatched away at source.

The Moores get a kick out of life along with their good friends Franz and Brigitte Beckenbauer.

Much later, Moore would have another reminder that you can never have enough credit in the bank, that you can never become bigger than a team, at least not in the mind of a winning manager like Ramsey.

When Moore became involved in the circus of the Bogotá bracelet affair in 1970, when he vehemently denied charges that he had removed the item from the glass case of a hotel shop, his greatest shock was that England flew away without him. Of course they left him in the care of British embassy officials and two senior men from the FA, but it was as though he had been removed from a comforting womb, an umbilical cord had been snipped. However, Ramsey's mission was to win the World Cup again in Mexico, a challenge which started a few days later.

No one in the England party doubted Moore's innocence, least of all Ramsey, and later there were conflicting theories, none of which involved the possibility of Moore's guilt. Perhaps it was a plot by the Colombians, or a prank by a young England player. Moore handled the crisis well, but he felt great strain, and, at times, terribly alone. But then he always knew that no level of celebrity insulated a man from essential loneliness when the pressure was at its greatest, and maybe he knew this more than any of his contemporaries. This would explain why his obsession with a good front, with flawlessness, was really his means of survival.

He got off the plane from Colombia late but unruffled. He continued to stand as tall as he could. It was tall enough to win, a few days later, the admiration of Pelé in a thunderous game in Guadalajara. It was simply the way he walked the line, the way he was and, right to the end, the way he would always be.

Covering the near post . . . the mature Moore in his ever-vigilant role with West Ham.
(Varley Picture Agency)

Moore waves farewell to the fans after his last league match for Fulham against Blackburn Rovers on 14 May 1977.
(*Colorsport*)

Bobby with wife Tina and children Roberta and Dean. (*Rex Features*)

Bobby builds sandcastles with his family's help. (*Rex Features*)

How they grow. Bobby with Roberta, now 27, in 1993.

Stephanie and Bobby going to a Buckingham Palace garden party. *(Alpha/Richard Chambury)*

Friend of the famous . . .
Moore relaxes with film
star Michael Caine. (*Rex
Features*)

A meeting of football
minds . . . Moore with
current England manager
Graham Taylor.

The Boys of '66 gather again. Moore, with World Cup in hand, celebrates the 25th anniversary of victory in 1991. *From the left:* Gerry Byrne, Ray Wilson, Moore, Ian Callaghan, Jack Charlton and Geoff Hurst.

World Cup heroes, 25 years on. *From the left:* George Cohen, Ray Wilson, Bobby Charlton and Bobby Moore. (*Syndication International*)

The shrine to Bobby Moore at Upton Park only a couple of days after his death. (*Syndication International*)

West Ham commemorated Bobby's death at that game on 6 March. His famous No. 6 shirt was re-created as a floral tribute and carried on to the pitch by Martin Peters and Geoff Hurst. They were led out by Ron Greenwood.

CHAPTER NINE

A SUPERSTAR AT HOME

In the winter before the golden summer of Bobby Moore, when he became England's first World Cup-winning captain and was immediately enshrined as a national hero, something remarkable happened to the status of the professional footballer. He leaped beyond the confines of the stadium, burst out of the sports page. No longer was he a muddied oaf, a Saturday afternoon diversion for the working man. Suddenly, he modelled clothes, was lionised by showbiz types. He was sometimes mocked on trendy satire shows – 'I've just opened a boutique, Brian' they tended to have him saying – but he didn't really care, because if he was very good at what he did, or more importantly if he had an 'image', he was living a life which great players could not have dreamed of just a decade before.

Bobby gets measured by Jean Fraser for his exhibition at Madame Tussaud's.

Men like Tommy Lawton and Wilf Mannion used to ride buses and shop at Burton's. Now, the professional footballer drove a flash car,

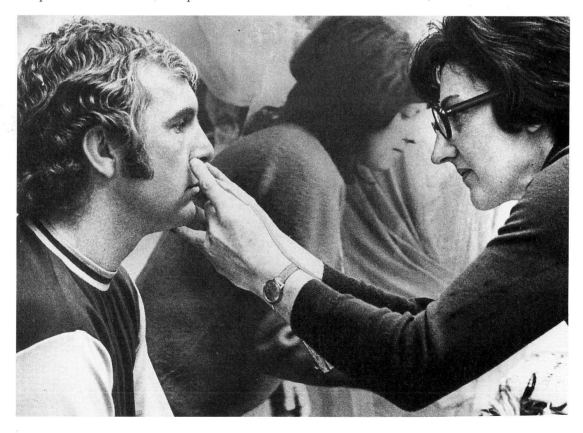

Tina shows those model girl looks.

(Right) And this outfit was designed by her husband.

bought Italian suits and took holidays in Benidorm. Also, quite often, he drank rum and coke. No experience expressed this sudden change of lifestyle more dramatically than that of George Best in that winter before the rise of Bobby Moore.

One day he was an extremely talented young player from a council estate in Belfast, a rather shy teenager negotiating marginal celebrity in a city always interested in its football players, the next he was the fifth Beatle. He certainly looked the part: handsome, dark-haired, a little soulful. And then his play exploded like a battery of fireworks. One night in Lisbon, in the appropriately named Estadio da Luz – Stadium of Light – he single-handedly destroyed the great team Benfica. He returned to a flood of flashbulbs and TV cameras. His life rapidly slipped out of control.

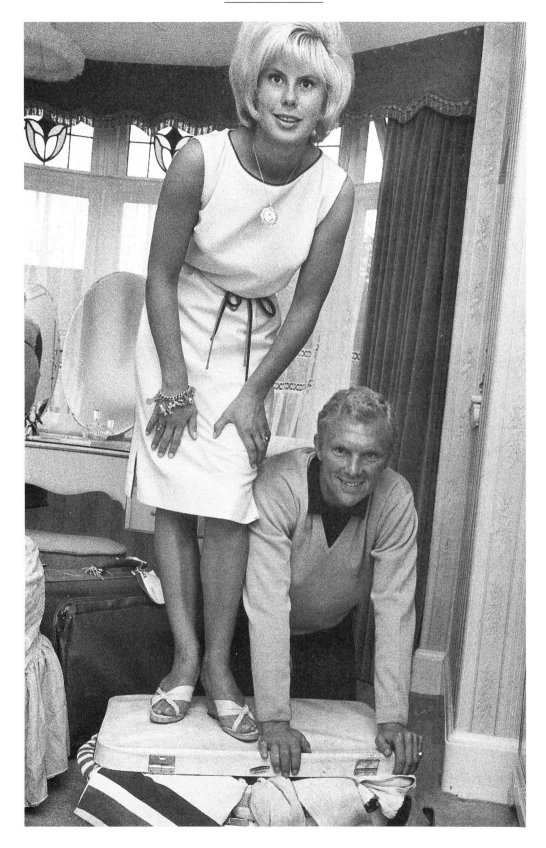

Moore was in a better position to handle his sudden elevation to huge celebrity. At the age of 20, he had married Christina ('Tina') Dean in the Church of St Clement's in Ilford. It was a white wedding and there was a nice 'do' afterwards – at the Valentine Hotel.

Bobby Moore had secured his base in life, marrying a girl who had entranced him one night at the Ilford Palais. She turned down several requests from him for a dance, but doggedly Moore pursued his goal. When they started off, their chances of success in marriage were no better or no worse than the hundreds of nice young couples who that year walked down the aisle at the Church of St Clement's. They had their rows, some quite furious, one of the most explosive of them coming on their honeymoon in Majorca. But then everyone rows on their honeymoon.

The real trouble, though it was a trouble that they dealt with for the best part of 20 years, was that, two years into their marriage, the status of their union changed as profoundly as that of Bobby's calling. He changed from football artisan to golden boy, an icon of the 1960s, a young man with whom prime minister Harold Wilson would never

Tina models Bobby's 1970 England shirt.

(Left) Bobby and Tina pack for West Ham's trip to New York in 1963.

miss a photo opportunity, someone suddenly befriended, symbolically enough by James Bond himself, actor Sean Connery. Bobby Moore was suddenly a prince. So Tina was seen as a princess, a 'model' and what they had was no longer a normal marriage, but they had to live up to a fairytale. Then, in the mid-70s, the fairytale ended: businesses went bust, the football came to an end. It's hard coming out of a fairytale and back into real life and the marriage followed the businesses and the football.

Tina lives in Florida now, and has not re-married.

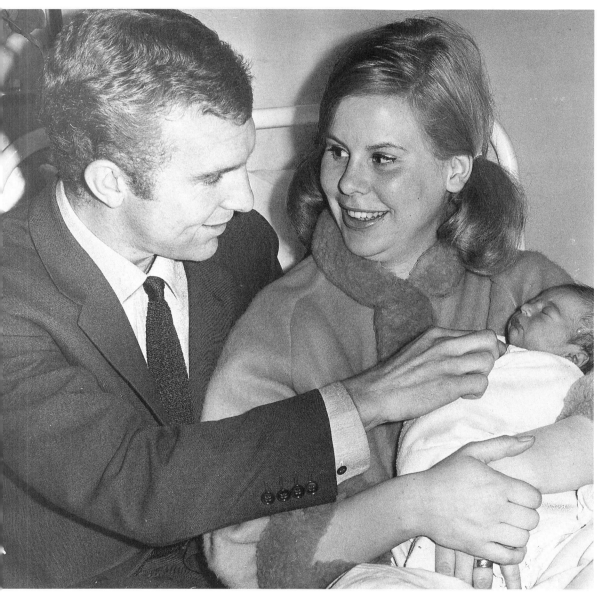

A few years after their split, when he was living with Stephanie, whom he would marry when he knew that he was terminally ill, Bobby and Tina met by chance on a London tube. A friend travelling with Moore braced himself but he reports, 'There was no hint of bitterness. Their marriage had run its course, they shared two children whom they loved, Roberta and Dean, and now they were like old friends who hadn't seen each other for a long time. The gales had blown out and now they were very calm in each other's company. They asked about each other and then Tina got off at her stop and for a little while Bobby didn't say anything. Such a big part of his life had just got off the tube.'

A famous player of Moore's generation, one who strenuously avoided the pitfalls of celebrity, says, 'I didn't know Tina personally, but sometimes I saw her being

Dean makes four in 1968. Note the boots.

It's a girl ... Tina and Bobby with day-old Roberta in January 1965.

interviewed, and from time to time she got quite a lot of publicity and I worried about that, because it is such an unnatural situation. Tina was a pretty girl, but it just happened she married a nice young guy she met at the Ilford Palais. When she first met him, when she married him, football players were no big deal, and their situation changed so much. In the normal way, a girl like Tina wouldn't have been exposed to such attention, and that has to change people, put strains on them. Expectations are created and it can put a lot of pressure on a relationship.'

In the yellowing pages of one of the heavy Sundays, one of those papers which, pre-1966, wouldn't have dreamed of interviewing the wife of a football player, there is a 1969 interview which ends poignantly enough with this quote from Tina: 'We have spells when everything is lovely, then we might row. We don't bicker, we'll have a terrible to-do and get it all over. Just spiteful things you regret afterwards.

'I've been lucky in marriage inasmuch as I got a nice person. Bobby kind of grows on you. I love him more now than when we were first married. He's very loyal and sincere, not only to me but other people. He's just a lovely person, and he's not big-headed, rather the reverse.

'We blend well – I'm happy, Bobby's happy. I just think things are marvellous. Please God, they go on as they are.'

The family Moore relax at Torremolinos.

But they couldn't go on forever. Bobby couldn't play football forever and he was too trusting for business.

When Tina said she hoped the marvellous things would go on forever they were living in a mock Tudor house in Chigwell. Five years later, in 1974, they moved up the hill and built a house Bobby described as the 'home of our dreams' in the posh enclave of Morlands.

Biographer Jeff Powell painted a picture of material wellbeing, of a seamless life of expensive things, of a banishment of all those imperatives that bedevil the calculations of the working class: the need to pay bills, to scrimp a holiday, to change the furniture.

He reported that the Moores paid £100,000 for their custom-built house and went on, 'By way of reward, they approach the new house through elegant white pillars, dine sumptuously behind rich velvet drapes, relax in deep sofas in a large cool lounge, dispense hospitality in Bobby's favourite room, his bar, and climb a grand curve of stairs to the pretty master suite which dominates the quiet complex of bedrooms and bathrooms. Tina has domestic help, notably in the fully gadgeted kitchen from which she is always promising herself to produce a Cordon Bleu meal, dabbles in charity work, takes care to look the part as Mrs Bobby Moore, steers the children through everything from riding lessons to the best education money can buy, lunches with friends, holidays in an assortment of sunspots and says, "It's been a hard life".

'Anticipating the public wince at the remark, she hurries on to the qualification, "A good life, yes, but still a hard life. There have been a lot of pressures. Not enough privacy. More time apart than we would like. Whatever Bobby's got he's earned the hard way. He's been on show almost every minute of the day. It has put us under pressure. After getting on for 15 years of marriage the miracle is that we still like each other".'

But Bobby and Tina were moving towards the end of the fairytale and Tina was right; it was, if not a miracle, a considerable balancing act they achieved on the way from the Ilford Palais to the heights of Chigwell. She had always been candid, describing their initial romance in terms that Barbara Cartland would never have recognised. It was more the detail of a social document.

'I first met Bobby when I was 16. We used to go to the same dance place. I had quite a few boyfriends at the time and I didn't take much notice of him. I suppose he was keener than I was – he was only 17 and hadn't many girlfriends. The first times he asked me out, I didn't turn up. Then, once, I was with my mother and I saw him in the milk bar and I pointed him out and she said, "Oh, he looks nice". So I thought, "Well yes…" He was a bit put-off by then, so I had to sort of go and say, "Hello, how are you?"

'I'd known him for three months when we started going steady. I'd just left school and he'd started playing for West Ham. I didn't realise how good he was then and, quite frankly, it wouldn't have impressed me. I liked him because he was a sincere person and good looking … and all my girlfriends liked him, and that helped. We used to meet every night except Friday – that was hairwashing night.

'The first year we were married was diabolical. It was a wonder we came through. I'd always been spoilt – I was an only child, Bobby was an only child – and we found it difficult. I wasn't used to doing anything for myself. I'd be reduced to tears by things like ironing Bobby's shirts. I drove myself mad with housework. We've both levelled down a bit now.

'We used to go to the theatre or the cinema and eat at Lyon's Corner House and take

Bobby and Tina on holiday in Athens in 1972.

the tube home. Now we go to Aretusa's or Anabel's or the White Elephant. We like to try out new places...'

Bobby confessed to a friend that going to tell his mother, Doris, that he was leaving Tina was one of the hardest things he ever did. She had long been a widow and when her electrician husband Robert died, the life of her only son and his family was her consuming interest. She idolised Bobby. He had brought her so much pride, more than she could ever have imagined when she gave birth to Robert Frederick at Upney Hospital. He had always been a credit to her and her hard-working husband.

Once Malcolm Allison, the senior pro at West Ham who had taken Bobby under his wing, came to their little house in Waverley Gardens, Barking, which was in fact a side street rather lacking in the promised flora off the busy River Road. He said that rather than sign for West Ham and take the paltry terms then offered to aspiring footballers, as a preliminary to a maximum wage of £20 a week, he should go off and play for a team in Ireland. Allison, who would later unsuccessfully argue against his protégé's early marriage, said this would give Bobby a good financial start in life. He could play a season with a League of Ireland club, then come home to receive a lump sum, perhaps as much as £10,000, to sign for an English team. The Moores were rather shocked. West Ham was Bobby's club. They thought he should do things the traditional way.

When, more than 20 years later, Moore went to his mother to say that his marriage was over she was as shocked as he had fearfully anticipated. She wept. She talked about family life. But Bobby was adamant, perhaps in a way that she had never seen before. He said he regretted that the marriage was over, as there had been good times and he didn't want to hurt the children, but he had found someone he loved, someone he knew would make him happy. Mrs Moore relented. She had been impressed by the cool force of her son's statement. It came after much agonising, and many nights of anguish in the heart of a man who would never cease wanting to do the right thing.

The woman who provoked in Bobby Moore the most troubling, and profound, decision of his life was Susan 'Stephanie' Parlane-Moore, a senior stewardess of British Airways. She was 33 when she met Bobby in 1983. By then he was no longer an icon of the game of football. He was manager of little Southend United, but, as long as he lived, Bobby Moore would be bigger than any station he had to take, in or out of football.

When he married Tina Dean, his wedding notice appeared in the *Walthamstow Guardian*. But when he left the family home in Essex and moved to Stephanie's cottage in Surrey, the world heard the news from a sensation-dealing tabloid. The headline screamed, 'Bobby Moore's "potty" for airgirl beauty.' It was the kind of banner Bobby Moore had spent half a lifetime seeking to avoid. But when it happened, he knew that it was right. Soon after Moore's death, a friend said to the grieving Stephanie, 'You had such a short time.'

'No,' she replied. 'We had ten wonderful years.'

In many ways, they were the toughest years of his life. It was clear he would never be a success in the lower rungs of football. He had no preparation for the scuffling nature of the job; he had lived his football on the high ground, and it was hard to operate with players of lesser talent – not because of arrogance, or any lack of love for the game or admiration for anyone who did his best, but because for 20 years, Moore had seen, as clearly as any player in the history of the game, the weaknesses of even great players. He had, after all, once played the great Pelé to a standstill. He

With Stephanie, the new girl in his life, in 1987.

moved from Southend to a Sunday tabloid, and then to a radio station. He did it with immense personal dignity, and if he had deep strength, if it seemed that nothing could break Bobby Moore, his friends said it had so much to do with Stephanie Parlane-Moore.

'They were wonderful together,' reports Malcolm Allison. 'I was told she put toothpaste on his brush – and I could believe it.'

When she had a short-haul flight, perhaps to Madrid, she would insist he came with her. She took him to see the paintings at the Prado, and they walked in the Retiro Park. At last Bobby Moore had entered a new world, one in which he didn't feel any pressure to perform an act or to maintain a front. It was as though he had learned to stop running, to stop tackling life and let it flow around him. He was calmer after going through the storm of his break-up with Tina. It was her gift to him, and those who knew him best say it was the greatest he ever received.

CHAPTER TEN
NEW CAREERS

Flicking through the pages of Bobby Moore's life, you find a most poignant chapter. It is the one which deals with his assumptions about how it would be after football. He seemed to be looking at the front of a chocolate box, but inside the wrapping there was a very harsh reality indeed. It was one for which nothing in his life, no more than any footballer's, had prepared him.

As a professional footballer, he operated in a time-warp, detached from the workaday implications of the real world. When he went into business, he discovered the place where those realities come to rest; a place where what you did yesterday doesn't mean a thing, where the only real imperative is to make a pound. Business people and football people operate on different planets. One planet – the football one – has an atmosphere which sustains fantasy. The other is friendly only to those who understand the bottom line of profit and loss. Here, fantasies simply shrivel to nothing.

This is why, when a football man and a businessman collide, there can be only one winner, unless the businessman for a while puts aside his most basic instincts and acts not on behalf of his own profit or loss but for the good of the football man. This happens from time to time, but it didn't happen to Bobby Moore. It happens because sometimes the businessman sees in the football man something he has lacked in his own life – glamour, perhaps, public acclaim, and so there is a trade-off. The businessman gains his goal of reflected glory.

The football world is filled with cases of men who came from the dusty corridors of commercial success, and total anonymity beyond their own business, to the warm glow of public recognition as chairmen of beloved football clubs. And the football man gains benefit from the businessman's acumen.

Those football men who have felt the benefit of such a relationship look around at former teammates who have lost their money and their hopes and they realise quite how lucky they have been. This luck didn't come to Bobby Moore. He was one of the casualties. It was a terrible reversal of fortune; the shattering of an assumption of financial well-being which was supported wherever he sought advice.

In 1970, a Sunday newspaper, noting the steady growth of the professional football profile in business, ordered up a report on Moore's financial standing and his future prospects. The figures seem quaint now, but it is still intriguing reading. It paints a picture

of unstoppable good fortune.

'Bobby Moore, aged 29, admits that he is not a millionaire. But he would like to be. "If it's possible to make a million out of soccer, I would like to be the first to do it," he says.

More friends for Bobby's book ... Elton John, Joe Bugner and Gerry Francis again.

'Moore, one of soccer's first £100-a-week players when the ceiling wage of £20 was lifted, currently earns between £7,000 and £8,000 in wages playing for West Ham. Modest, perhaps, compared with the estimated £20,000 that George Best earns. But with business interests in advertising, modelling, clothes manufacturing, sports books and syndicated sports columns, Moore's earnings per year are estimated at treble his actual pay for playing football.

'This year he expects an additional £4,000 to £5,000 in World Cup perks, from the cup pool itself and sales of the current hit parade record "Back Home", a song rendered by the England footballers.

'The son of a Barking electrician – Moore's parents still live in the terraced house where he was brought up – he has been an ad-man's dream since he first emerged as a promising player. With his blond hair and good looks, he has the physique and handsome features of a Nordic warrior. Natural attributes which he soon turned into hard cash. His face peered down from billboards advertising a hairdressing product.

'Then television began to woo him. First it was a series. "Look in at the Local," currently he's selling Bisto. The fees are thought to add up to as much as £10,000 a year. The Ford Motor Company have him driving their cars. Moore changes his cars regularly. He has owned a Rover and Mercedes, but is more often seen in a Jaguar or Ford.

The trappings of success ... a Daimler Jag.

(Left) Filmstar Moore with Sylvester Stallone (left) and Michael Caine at the premier of their film Escape to Victory in 1981.

'He owns a sportswear shop opposite the West Ham ground. It's managed by his wife Tina's stepfather. Business is brisk.

'He is in the rag trade. He is co-director of a firm producing suede and leather goods, with its head office in Aldgate. The boom in leather clothes has meant an overwhelming stream of orders. Bobby spends a lot of time working at the firm.

'He also has an interest in a Hatton Garden jewellers. He has modelled men's shirts, ties and even swimwear. His writing interests increase yearly. At 29, he has already written one autobiography and another will be published shortly. A weekly newspaper column brings him in approximately £1,000 a year and a World Cup cartoon strip is currently syndicated to papers in all parts of the country. The *Bobby Moore Annual*, a coaching manual and his own *Book of Soccer* bring him in a steady supply of royalties.

'He is constantly being offered directorships and is looking for a bigger house than the one in Chigwell's Manor Road "smart set" bought three years ago. Moore considers he can play for another eight or nine years if all goes well. But he is preparing for it to be shorter. "I want to make sure my family and I can afford to live as comfortably when I finish football as they do now. If that is an ambition, they can say I'm ambitious."'

**The sports shop opposite
Upton Park.**

Moore was right that his career might be shorter than he hoped, but only marginally. And the forlorn truth was that, of all his projections and hopes for a secure future, this was just about the only thing he got right. Business drew in Moore, the football man with the golden touch, but it refused to deliver its promises. Moore lost money, relentlessly. The leather boom faded and his partner, Freddie Harrison, went bankrupt. The company went into liquidation with debts of £73,697. In 1975, his East End pub, the Old Black Bull in Stratford High Street, burned down on the eve of its re-opening as 'Mooro's and there was talk of arson. Other investments went down – notably one in the Woolston Hall Country Club in Essex, which crashed with debts of more than £500,000.

Moore had been ably supported by his agent Jack Turner, who had submitted the first scouting report on Moore all those years ago. He was a man of conservative instincts and impeccable standards who took a straight ten per cent from outside work he handled for the young man he had admired so much while working as a financial adviser on behalf of West Ham United. Turner advised against investing in the country club. But Moore and Tina had been attracted by the glamour of the country club. A fellow investor was Sean Connery.

Said Moore, 'It seemed perfect for the area and the deal seemed tremendous. We had the house valued at £500,000 and the total cost of the project was only £50,000. There were 26 acres of land only 12 miles from London and we all knew we lived in a rich area where you had to queue up to get a table in the local restaurants. What we didn't know, between us, was the slightest thing about catering or organising a club of this kind. The great problem was that, with the exception of the restaurant, disco and bars, we spent a fortune on facilities which didn't bring a penny piece. And we had bought the best of everything, from the teaspoons upwards.'

Moore turns publican with The Three Horseshoes at Spelbrook, Essex.

The club, the pub, the leatherworks – they were the accumulating evidence that Bobby Moore was miscast in the role of the businessman.

'A lot of footballers had gone down Bobby's road,' says Johnny Giles, a contemporary player who at the age of 31 lost all his savings in an insurance business. 'I spent years paying off the damage, trying to get straight,' said Giles. 'Fortunately, I had a few decent earning years left in the game, but it was hard and painful work…'

Giles, the field general of the great Leeds United, was once accused by another player's wife of having 'tunnel vision', of being so preoccupied with football he had no sense of a

wider world. Giles, a well-read, articulate man, was outraged. Then he went home and thought about it and concluded that the player's wife had been right.

'The trouble is,' says Giles, 'that when lads come out of school and go into normal jobs, they encounter the real world soon enough. In football, you enter a kind of

Still fit after all these years … Bobby with old adversary Uwe Seeler of West Germany in the 1985 re-run of the World Cup final.

(Right) The last match … Bobby turns out at Elland Road, Leeds, in a game between England and West Germany to aid victims of the Bradford fire.

cocoon. I spent 20-odd years in a football dressing room and you don't get involved in too many discussions about the state of the economy or whether the City of London or Wall Street is bullish or nervous or whatever. You're more likely to be playing a practical joke on one of the lads, or fixing a golf game. Football is a fantasy and football players are locked into it. Most of them sooner or later have to walk out of a football ground for the last time; they have to face up to the fact that life will never be quite the same again.'

Giles encountered this reality with some force one day at an airport bar. Someone came up to him and said, 'Didn't you use to be Johnny Giles?' Giles replied, 'As a matter of fact, I still am.'

But he knew well enough that things were different, as Bobby Moore did, when the business turned to ashes and when the cheering stopped. 'When a kid becomes a football player he is a wedded to a dream', adds Giles. 'He doesn't see life beyond the game, he rushes along this tunnel, and then suddenly he comes out at the other end. Nothing has

prepared him for what happens then...'

Bobby Moore's career was one of the great glories of football and perhaps also one of the great lessons. Because of his character, because of his natural dignity, he didn't go the way of so many of the disillusioned. He kept his standards, he rode the blows, and he fashioned a life from what looked, inevitably for a while, a disturbing void.

When his career was just about done, and when the weight of business failure oppressed him, he said, 'Hell, I'd like my playing career all over again. Maybe I've got

In the manager's chair at Southend United.

(Left) Bobby tries his hand at management with Oxford City. (Below left) Team talk at Oxford.

nothing left to prove as a player. Maybe I proved myself the best at my business for 12 years, non-stop, and you don't have to go on proving that forever, but I still wish I could... I wish I could go on forever.'

It is the grim realisation for almost every pro, that first grasping of the fact that his time is almost up. And who had ever had such a time as Moore? Pelé, no doubt. Johan Cruyff, the golden Dutchman, but he never won a World Cup. Franz Beckenbauer, 'the emperor' of West Germany, is perhaps closest to Moore in footballing experience. He led

West Germany to the World Cup with that same Moore-like hauteur and certainty. But, unlike Moore, Beckenbauer was relentlessly celebrated by his national football association. Eventually, he was put in charge of the national team. It put him on to the high ground of earning potential in football management.

Bobby Moore never got such a call, a fact which makes poignant a remark he made when his playing days were ending: 'When I was playing I never thought much about running my own team, but now that prospect excites me. I can see it as an extension of playing. It would have to be right. I wouldn't want to start at the bottom all over again, scuffling about in the lower divisions. But the right challenge, at the right club, great.'

It wasn't great. He had to scuffle at

The way we were ... Bobby and Alan Mullery dress up for a charity match.

Oxford City, then Southend United. He did it without public complaint. He had won great victories in his career, but his fortune had changed and if he was a good winner, he proved that he could handle the reverse side as well as any man who ever played the game.

In all of this there was a great irony. As his playing days drew in, he wondered if there was any real future in the game, whether the wealth of it had drained away. He said, 'I was lucky enough to be around for the best years professional players have ever known in this country. From now on, there will be a handful of top men still earning good money.

But by and large, the economy of the game is becoming much tighter.'

The fact is that, if Bobby Moore had been born 20 years later, his business battles, his insomniac nights, would have been utterly avoidable. At an age when he told that Sunday newspaper that he would like to be football's first millionaire, that target would have been a molehill. His fortune would have been assured by a stroke of a pen. Roy Keane, the impressive young player of Nottingham Forest, recently signed a contract worth a reputed £250,000 a year – and into which was inserted a clause that he was free to consider other offers if they reached a certain scale. Bobby Moore would have settled for that when he became frustrated by the boundaries of Upton Park and the earning limits that now seem to belong not to other decades but to another age.

In the end, though, these are matters for the margins of Bobby Moore's life. He was never a businessman, never a man to measure too closely his own earning power and that of his rivals. He lived his life with the simple imperative of being the best at what he did, what he knew. What he knew was competing at the very highest level of the game. His old West Ham manager once regretted that his great player could not play all his games at Wembley. The point was well made. Moore was an adornment to the West Ham team down the years, but it was when he put on the white shirt of England that you saw the weight of his talent, the range of his command. He needed to be drawn out, to have his resources explored and tested. Business and commerce could never do that. Football was the place where he would always shine most brilliantly.

One of his old West Ham teammates commented: 'Players thought they could get away with Moore's lifestyle without copying his discipline, that he would always be around to bale them out, which was true, but this was why he came to have a certain contempt for some players. Bobby could not understand people who failed to take responsibility for their own lives.'

So he would never make it as businessman of the year. Had he known, he might have smiled in his rueful way and said: 'Well, you win some and you lose some.'

The comfort for those who loved and admired Bobby Moore is that he won all the ones that mattered. Something that mattered deeply was the respect of Pelé, the world's most famous and admired football player. When Moore died, Pelé said: 'Moore was my friend, the finest, the most honourable defender I ever played against.'

It was the last entry in the profit and loss account of Bobby Moore. And it said it all – all that really mattered.

TRIBUTES
TO A GREAT MAN

Bobby Moore's greatest inspiration, Sir Alf Ramsey, and mightiest opponent, Pelé, joined to mourn the man they called the best. Ramsey was famous for keeping his feelings to himself. But emotion took over as he faced up to the death of his World Cup-winning captain, with the admission:

> *'It was one of the saddest days of my life.'* The 73-year-old soccer knight, said: *'He was my captain and my right-hand man. Bobby was the heartbeat of the England team, the king of the castle, my representative on the field.'*

The rest of the soccer world, and all of Moore's colleagues from his World Cup victory in 1966, queued to pay tribute. But nobody was closer to him than Ramsey, who appointed a 23-year-old Moore to lead England in 1964.

> *'He made things work on the pitch. I had the deepest trust in him as a man, as a captain, as a confidant and as a footballer,'* he said.
> *'We would not have won the World Cup if Bobby Moore had not been our skipper. For four years, he was not only the best defender in the world but also the best captain. Just ask Pelé. He held him in higher esteem than any other player in Europe and my heart goes out to everybody who admired and respected him as much as I did.'*

Brazilian legend Pelé was on a business trip to Uruguay when informed of his old adversary's death and he said:

> *'Words cannot sum up the grief I feel for my great friend. He was one of the world's finest defenders and a great sportsman. The shirt he wore against me in the 1970 World Cup in Mexico is my prize possession. Besides being a fellow player, he was my friend. My thoughts and prayers are with his family.'*

Franz Beckenbauer, the former West German captain and manager, said:

> *'Bobby Moore was always a football idol for me as a young player. I looked up to him. I was so proud that I could play against him and later he became a great friend. The news of his illness stunned me. He was too young.'*

Hans Tilkowski, the German goalkeeper in 1966, added:

'I was in London at the weekend before he died helping to make a film about the World Cup final. I tried to visit Bobby but it was late to let me see him. He was a great sportsman and one of the best men I knew.'

Ron Greenwood, the West Ham manager who groomed Moore for stardom at the Upton Park footballing academy, said:

'Bobby was an example to everyone. He was everything that was clean and good. It's so very, very sad. He was so young. I feel deeply for him and his family.

'He had a bearing about him. He was born to be a leader, and there can't be enough of a tribute to him in a football sense. He was everything that was good in the game. He was dedicated. He was gifted. He had such presence.'

Greenwood, who made Moore his teenage captain at West Ham, continued:

'He stood out so early. He had a thirst for knowledge. He wanted to be the best and that was what he became. I first knew him as a 17-year-old when I was manager of England's Youth team. I made him captain. Then he played under me when I was manager of the England Under-23s and, of course, I joined up with him when I became manager of West Ham.

'He was due to come to West Ham the Sunday before he died, but Trevor Brooking told me he didn't want to embarrass anyone. He must have been very ill then.'

Bobby Charlton shared the 1966 triumph with Moore and then succeeded him as England captain. He said:

'I am terribly shocked even though I knew he was ill. I know that all football people in the country will miss him. He was a gentle man, he always did things with dignity and a bit of style – he was the most stylish of players. He was a great footballer but I prefer to remember him as a person. He was a lovely man.'

Martin Peters, with Geoff Hurst one of the West Ham triumvirate in the England World Cup-winning team, said:

'I'm totally shocked. I had no idea Bobby was so ill and we had some great days together. I last saw him before Christmas, but spoke to him only ten days ago when he asked me to take part in a charity match for Malcolm Allison. That was typical of the man, thinking of others before himself.

'It was about three days before the news broke about his illness and he didn't say anything to me about it. We sent him a card wishing him all the best – but didn't like to intrude too much. He was more than just a friend and colleague for many years. He was a man of tremendous character. It is difficult to talk about his contribution to football at a time like this – but he was a great.'

Former Fulham manager Alec Stock gave Moore his last big match, ironically against West Ham, in the 1975 FA Cup final. He commented:

'Bobby was marvellous in every way. The perfect professional, never late for training, never moaned about aches or pains or feeling tired. He only ever wanted to do one thing and that was to play football. For me, he did that better than any Englishman has ever done.'

George Best was a teammate of Moore at Fulham and he was in tears as he said:

'Bobby was the greatest of players and one of the greatest men I knew. I have lost a very close and very, very dear friend.'

Ex-England captains Gary Lineker and Bryan Robson added their tributes.

'Bobby Moore was a colossus of the modern game, not only because of his playing achievements, but the dignity with which he conducted himself throughout his career,' said Lineker.

Bryan Robson added:

'He was England's great captain and when I was growing up Bobby Moore was one of my first heroes. When I became England captain, I was asked what I wanted to achieve. I said just to emulate Bobby Moore, but I never could.'

David Platt said from Italy:

'Bobby was a great person in every sense, a footballer of intelligence and vision. I admired and respected him enormously. I was only six weeks old when Bobby lifted the World Cup and now, 26 years later, he saw his last game at Wembley and I was the captain. I shan't forget my night for so many reasons and that will obviously be one of them. You look at people who have been in the situation of captaining England and when you look at Bobby, he stood for everything you would like to be yourself.'

Moore was paid a massive tribute by the Players' Union when they renamed their annual Fair Play Trophy after the former England World Cup captain. The decision highlighted one of the characteristics that made the 51-year-old ex-West Ham defender a giant of the world game.

Gordon Taylor, chief executive of the Professional Footballers' Association, said:

'We felt it appropriate that our Fair Play award should be renamed the Bobby Moore Trophy and we have written to his widow Stephanie and family to express our deepest sympathy and ask if we can do just that. It's a tribute that we wish to make to one of the finest members of our Association. Bobby led from the front with dignity, skill, style and with a great sense of sportsmanship and fair play.'